HOW IT WORKS

EXPLORING THE
OCEANS

Stephen Hall

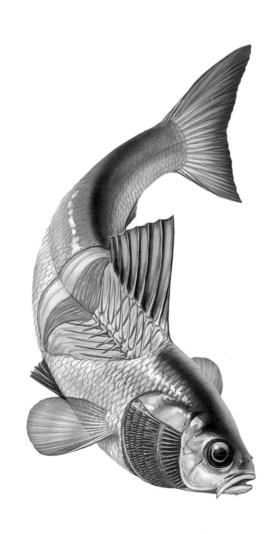

HORUS EDITIONS

Published by Horus Editions Limited
1st Floor, 27 Longford Street,
London NW1 3DZ

Copyright © 1998 Horus Editions Limited

Series editor Elizabeth Miles
Designed by Paul Richards and Jenny Fry
Illustrations by Jim Channell, David Hardy,
Sebastian Quigley, Steve Seymour,
Steve Weston and Gerald Witcomb
Additional research by Ivailo Grigorov

Printed in Singapore

HOW IT WORKS
CONTENTS

The Ocean Floor

THE EARTH'S thin surface layer is known as the crust. It is split into several pieces, called plates, that drift slowly on a lower layer of molten, denser rock. Two types of rock form these plates: continental and oceanic. Continental rock is about 40 kilometres thick, increasing to 70 kilometres under high mountain ranges. Oceanic rock is only about 6 kilometres thick. Beneath the oceans, oceanic rock is constantly forming at 'spreading ridges' where plates are pulling apart. Oceanic rock is always being destroyed in 'subduction zones', where it dips under a continental plate and melts.

Water fills up the great oceanic basins, but the amount of water varies over time. Today, sea levels are high enough to cover the lower parts of the continents. These submerged parts are called continental shelves.

AS MOUNTAINS ARE WORN DOWN BY THE WEATHER, MATERIAL IS CARRIED BY RIVERS INTO THE OCEAN

A SLOPE DOWN TO THE DEEP OCEAN FLOOR LIES AT THE EDGE OF A CONTINENT

LOW LYING LAND IS FLOODED BY THE OCEAN WHEN SEA LEVELS RISE

MOLTEN ROCK RISES AND THEN SETS HARD TO FORM THE CORE OF MOUNTAINS

OCEANIC CRUST SOMETIMES CONTINUES BELOW THE THICKER CONTINENTAL CRUST

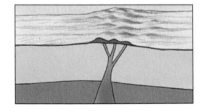
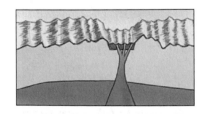
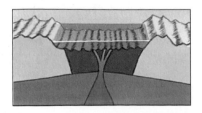

The birth of an ocean
Volcanic activity starts along a weak point in the Earth's crust (*top left*). As the crust splits and two or more plates drift apart a steep-sided valley is formed, like the Rift Valley of East Africa (*middle*). The valley floods, and over millions of years widens into an ocean (*bottom*). Long ago Africa and America split apart and the Atlantic Ocean filled the gap.

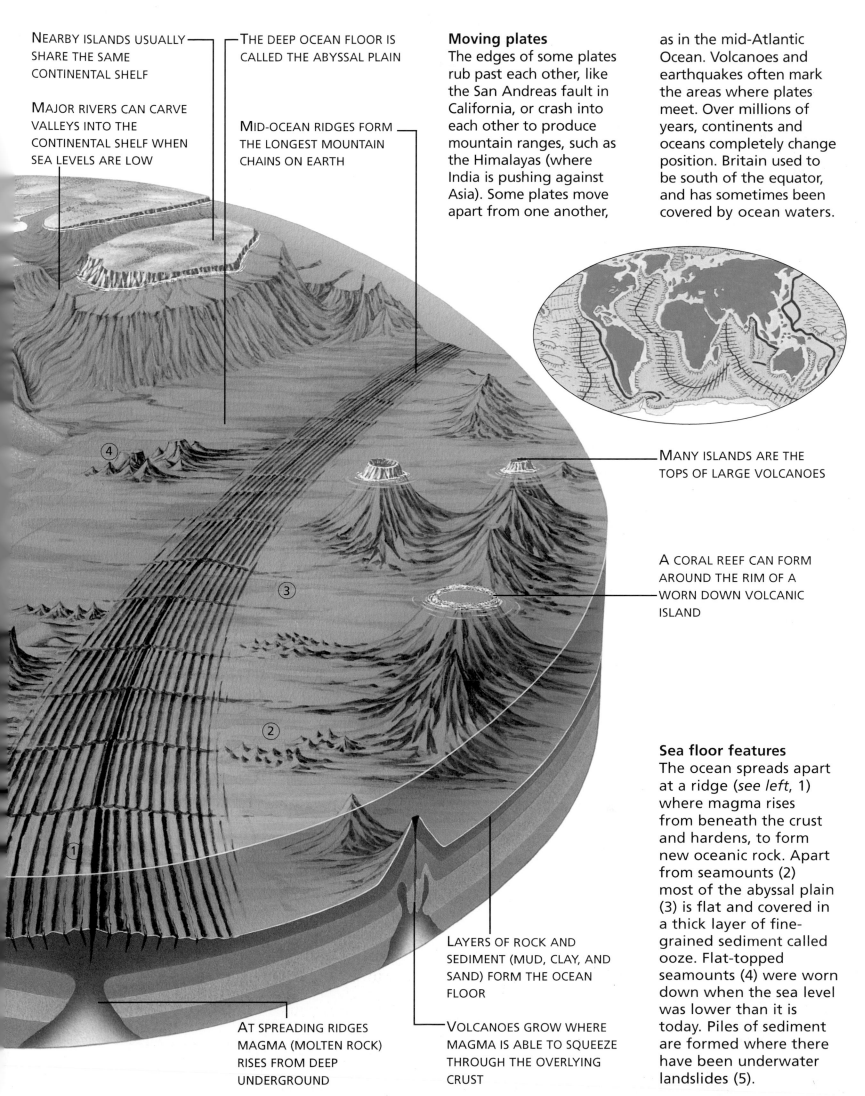

NEARBY ISLANDS USUALLY SHARE THE SAME CONTINENTAL SHELF

MAJOR RIVERS CAN CARVE VALLEYS INTO THE CONTINENTAL SHELF WHEN SEA LEVELS ARE LOW

THE DEEP OCEAN FLOOR IS CALLED THE ABYSSAL PLAIN

MID-OCEAN RIDGES FORM THE LONGEST MOUNTAIN CHAINS ON EARTH

Moving plates

The edges of some plates rub past each other, like the San Andreas fault in California, or crash into each other to produce mountain ranges, such as the Himalayas (where India is pushing against Asia). Some plates move apart from one another, as in the mid-Atlantic Ocean. Volcanoes and earthquakes often mark the areas where plates meet. Over millions of years, continents and oceans completely change position. Britain used to be south of the equator, and has sometimes been covered by ocean waters.

MANY ISLANDS ARE THE TOPS OF LARGE VOLCANOES

A CORAL REEF CAN FORM AROUND THE RIM OF A WORN DOWN VOLCANIC ISLAND

LAYERS OF ROCK AND SEDIMENT (MUD, CLAY, AND SAND) FORM THE OCEAN FLOOR

AT SPREADING RIDGES MAGMA (MOLTEN ROCK) RISES FROM DEEP UNDERGROUND

VOLCANOES GROW WHERE MAGMA IS ABLE TO SQUEEZE THROUGH THE OVERLYING CRUST

Sea floor features

The ocean spreads apart at a ridge (*see left*, 1) where magma rises from beneath the crust and hardens, to form new oceanic rock. Apart from seamounts (2) most of the abyssal plain (3) is flat and covered in a thick layer of fine-grained sediment called ooze. Flat-topped seamounts (4) were worn down when the sea level was lower than it is today. Piles of sediment are formed where there have been underwater landslides (5).

Tides

THE MOON orbits (travels around) the Earth, and together the Earth and Moon orbit the Sun. While this happens the gravitational forces of the Moon and Sun pull on the oceans, causing tides. The Moon has a more powerful effect on the tides as it is much closer to the Earth. It stretches the Earth's ocean waters into an oval shape, creating a tidal bulge on each side of the Earth. These tidal bulges are where high tides occur.

The usual tidal range, or difference between high- and low-water level, is 2–3 metres on open coastlines. Many things can affect the tidal range, including severe weather, the presence of land such as islands, friction of the tide against the sea floor, and wind direction. Complicated multiple tides can also occur when tidal cycles affect one another. The largest tidal ranges are where the shape of the coastline strengthens the tidal effects. Seas that are enclosed, such as the Mediterranean Sea, show a much smaller tidal range than the open oceans.

The effects of the Sun and Moon

Below you can see how the oceans bulge outward towards the Moon and Sun (the effects are exaggerated to make them clearer). When the Moon and Sun are at right angles (*pictures 1 and 3*) you can see the stronger pull of the Moon on the oceans. Because the Sun is pulling from a different direction the tidal bulges are less extreme and 'neap' tides occur. When the Moon and Sun are in line their forces combine and more extreme 'spring' tides occur (*2 and 4*). The greatest tides occur during the spring and autumn equinoxes, when the Sun is directly over the equator and most perfectly aligned with the Moon. Many plants and animals have adapted to take advantage of the tidal ranges.

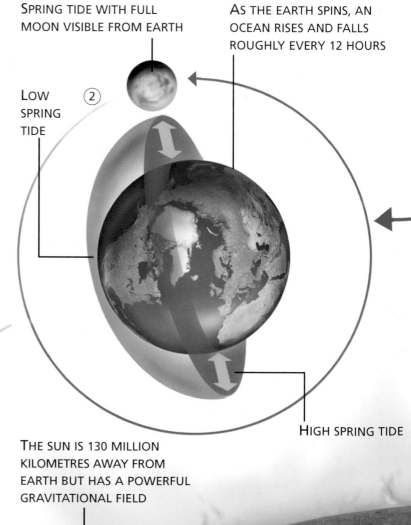

SPRING TIDE WITH FULL MOON VISIBLE FROM EARTH

AS THE EARTH SPINS, AN OCEAN RISES AND FALLS ROUGHLY EVERY 12 HOURS

LOW SPRING TIDE

②

HIGH SPRING TIDE

THE SUN IS 130 MILLION KILOMETRES AWAY FROM EARTH BUT HAS A POWERFUL GRAVITATIONAL FIELD

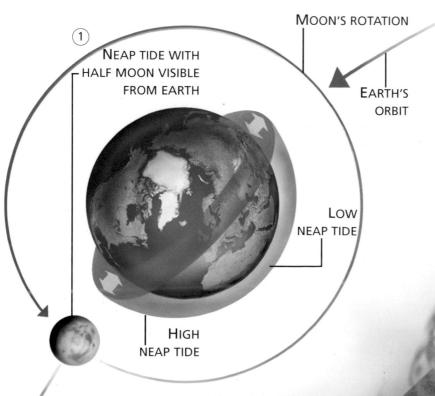

MOON'S ROTATION

①

NEAP TIDE WITH HALF MOON VISIBLE FROM EARTH

EARTH'S ORBIT

LOW NEAP TIDE

HIGH NEAP TIDE

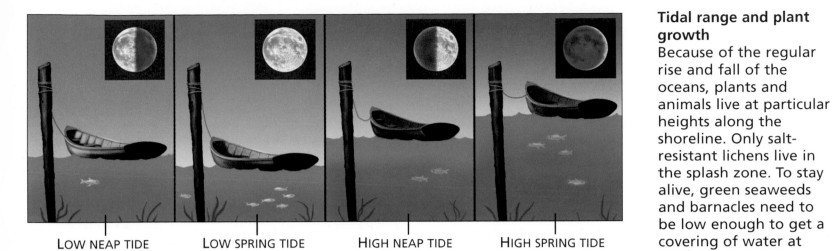

LOW NEAP TIDE   LOW SPRING TIDE   HIGH NEAP TIDE   HIGH SPRING TIDE

Tidal range and plant growth

Because of the regular rise and fall of the oceans, plants and animals live at particular heights along the shoreline. Only salt-resistant lichens live in the splash zone. To stay alive, green seaweeds and barnacles need to be low enough to get a covering of water at high tide.

Tidal ranges

The positions of the boat and views of the Moon show the differences between spring and neap tides.

At Full and New Moon, we get spring tides, when the tidal difference is great. At Half Moon the tidal difference is small.

LICHENS LIVE ABOVE THE HIGH TIDE MARK, IN THE SPLASH ZONE

HIGH TIDE WATERS REACH GREEN SEAWEED, LIMPETS, AND BARNACLES

BROWN SEAWEEDS LIVE NEAR THE LOW TIDE MARK, SO THEY ARE UNDERWATER MOST OF THE TIME

RED SEAWEEDS OFTEN GROW BELOW THE LOW TIDE MARK

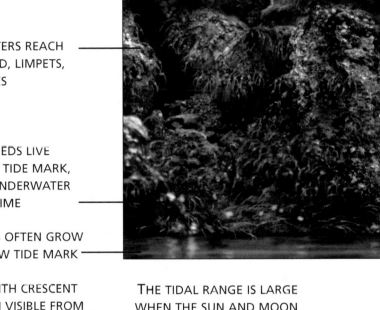

NEAP TIDE WITH HALF MOON VISIBLE FROM EARTH

③

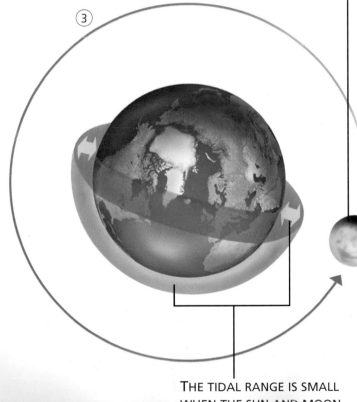

SPRING TIDE WITH CRESCENT OR NEW MOON VISIBLE FROM EARTH

THE TIDAL RANGE IS LARGE WHEN THE SUN AND MOON PULL FROM THE SAME DIRECTION

④

THE TIDAL RANGE IS SMALL WHEN THE SUN AND MOON ARE AT RIGHT ANGLES

Waves and Wind

THE EARTH is like a huge spinning ball, with a heat lamp – the Sun – shining over the equator. At the equator, ocean waters get warmer and move out towards the extreme northern and southern parts of the Earth (the North and South Poles). At the poles the water becomes cooler and flows back towards the equator to begin the cycle again. This is how currents of water move deep in the oceans. Surface currents are caused by winds, the spin of the Earth, and the position of land masses (*see below, right*).

Winds also cause waves as they blow over the surface of the sea. As shown below, the water itself does not move forward in a wave. The water particles only go round in a circle. It is the energy that this movement makes that moves forward with a wave.

The Beaufort Scale

The Beaufort Scale is used to describe the strength of the wind at sea. This system relies on signs that can be seen with the eye, rather than on scientific instruments, but is still a valuable warning of stormy seas.

0 calm, sea like a mirror
1 light air, small ripples
2 light breeze, small wavelets
3 gentle breeze, wave crests begin to break
4 moderate breeze, small waves and some 'white horses'
5 fresh breeze, frequent waves, many 'white horses'
6 strong breeze, large waves 3 metres high begin to form
7 near gale, rough sea with spray
8 gale, waves up to 6 metres high
9 strong gale, rough waves, up to 9 metres high
10 storm, visibility difficult, waves up to 12 metres high
11 violent storm, sea covered in foam, small ships lost to view between wave crests
12 hurricane, waves over 14 metres high, air filled with foam/spray.

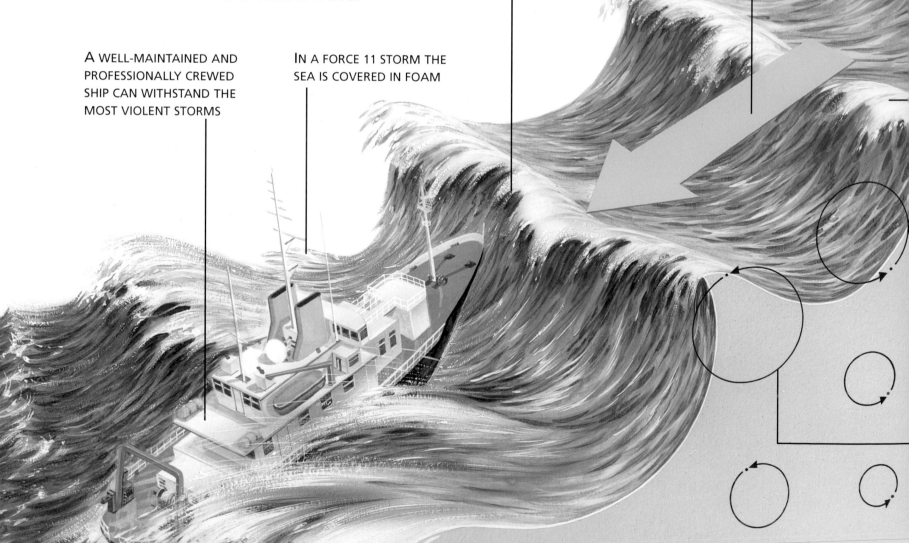

WAVE PEAKS ARE WHIPPED INTO FOAM BY A STRONG FORCE 8 GALE

WAVES WITH HEIGHTS OF MORE THAN 30 METRES HAVE BEEN RECORDED

A WELL-MAINTAINED AND PROFESSIONALLY CREWED SHIP CAN WITHSTAND THE MOST VIOLENT STORMS

IN A FORCE 11 STORM THE SEA IS COVERED IN FOAM

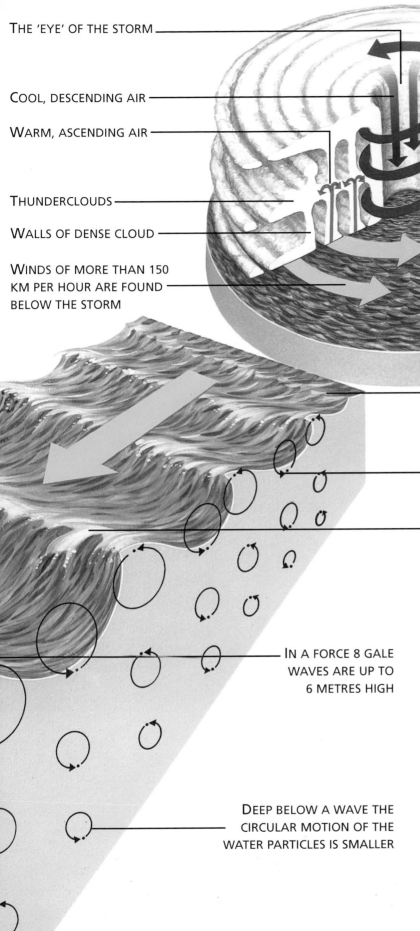

THE 'EYE' OF THE STORM

COOL, DESCENDING AIR

WARM, ASCENDING AIR

THUNDERCLOUDS

WALLS OF DENSE CLOUD

WINDS OF MORE THAN 150 KM PER HOUR ARE FOUND BELOW THE STORM

AIR SPIRALS IN TOWARDS THE 'EYE' OF STORM

Great storms

Tropical revolving storms (known as typhoons, hurricanes or cyclones) form over warm water and can reach 560–800 kilometres in diameter. Walls of dense cloud form rings around the centre of the storm as warm, moist air is drawn in and spirals rapidly upwards. The 'eye' (centre) of the storm is a calm area of cool, descending air. These storms cause tremendous damage if they pass over land, but soon die out as they move in from the coast.

LIGHT BREEZES CAUSE SMALL WAVELETS

AT THE END OF EACH WAVE, WATER PARTICLES ARE BACK WHERE THEY STARTED

AS WAVE HEIGHT INCREASES THE ANGLE OF THE CREST GETS STEEPER

IN A FORCE 8 GALE WAVES ARE UP TO 6 METRES HIGH

DEEP BELOW A WAVE THE CIRCULAR MOTION OF THE WATER PARTICLES IS SMALLER

Surface waters

The colours on the map below show the temperatures of land and ocean surface waters. The temperatures were picked up by a satellite as it orbited the Earth. Warm equatorial temperatures are shown in orange; cool polar temperatures are shown in green and blue.

The arrows on the map show the flow of surface currents (warm currents are in red; cold are in blue). These wind driven currents are swung to one side by the spin of the Earth, creating large circular currents in the oceans. All oceans are connected by currents at various depths. The currents have a great effect on climate. For example, warm waters from the Indian Ocean enter the Atlantic and move north, helping to keep northern Europe warm.

THE WATER PARTICLES IN THE WAVE MOVE IN A CIRCULAR PATTERN, BUT THE ENERGY OF THE WAVE MOVES FORWARDS

THE EQUATOR IS AN IMAGINARY LINE AROUND THE EARTH, LYING HALFWAY BETWEEN THE POLES

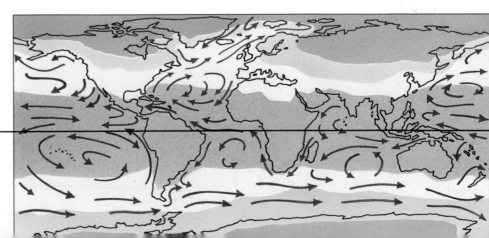

Coastlines

COASTS ARE where the land and sea do battle. Without humans becoming involved, the sea usually wins. The coastal land that survives the pounding of storm waves best is made of hard, volcanic rock; soft sandstone, on the other hand, is easily worn away. The slope of coastal rocks and any weaknesses in them that the ocean can make use of also influence the shape of the coastline.

Coasts are the most popular places for people to live, work, and take vacations. To preserve rapidly eroding coastlines engineers build sea defence works such as walls of concrete or stone. Beaches are sometimes preserved with walls or jetties called groynes. In some countries whole areas of low-lying land have been reclaimed from the sea by building walls called dykes, and then pumping away the seawater.

Large rivers preserve the coast because as they enter the sea, rivers deposit many tonnes of mud, stone, and sand onto the sea floor, building up natural sea defences.

Speed of erosion
How long can a coastline last? There are several things to take into account. In particular, the hardness of the rock, the fierceness of the sea, and the presence of sea-defences are critical.

Over many years sea levels change and this also effects how coastlines are eroded (worn down). For example, thousands of years ago areas of land were covered in ice that eventually melted. Since the weight of the ice was lifted, the land has slowly sprung back upwards. This accounts for the ancient beaches found high above the present sea level in many places. Where rocks under a coastline are now sinking, the sea can flood an area that was once dry land.

COVES ARE FORMED WHEN THE SEA OPENS A GAP THROUGH A NECK OF HARD ROCK INTO SOFTER ROCK BEHIND

LIKE THE SEA, A RIVER WILL FLOW THROUGH ROCK WEAKENED BY A GEOLOGICAL FAULT

IN SHELTERED AREAS SAND DUNES FORM

ABANDONED HOUSES ARE LOST OVER A RAPIDLY ERODING CLIFF

DEBRIS WILL SOON BE WORN DOWN INTO SAND BY WAVES

Coastal waves
Waves become shorter and steeper as they approach the coast. This is because the circular motion of water particles within the wave gets pushed upwards as the wave is influenced by the sloping sea floor. Once it has reached its maximum height, the wave breaks. The water then sweeps back out to sea, as backwash.

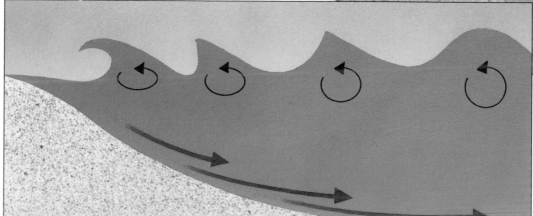

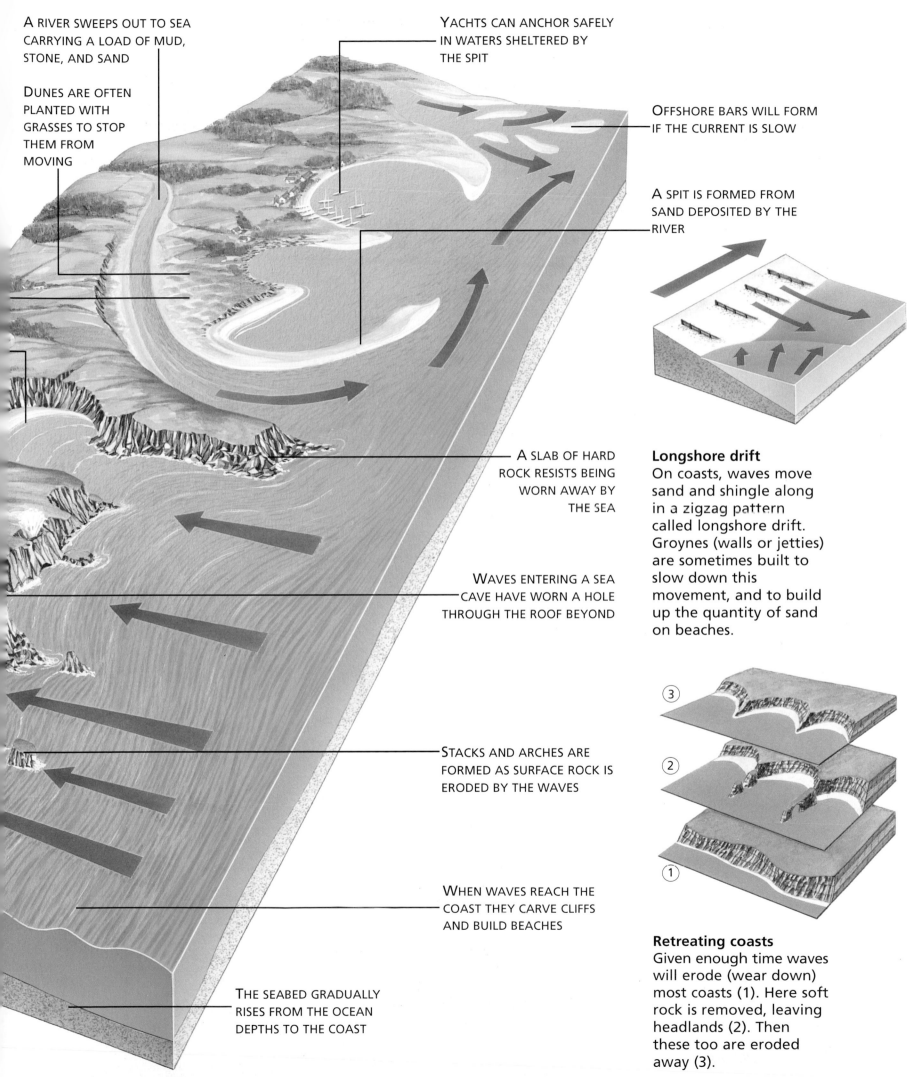

A RIVER SWEEPS OUT TO SEA CARRYING A LOAD OF MUD, STONE, AND SAND

DUNES ARE OFTEN PLANTED WITH GRASSES TO STOP THEM FROM MOVING

YACHTS CAN ANCHOR SAFELY IN WATERS SHELTERED BY THE SPIT

OFFSHORE BARS WILL FORM IF THE CURRENT IS SLOW

A SPIT IS FORMED FROM SAND DEPOSITED BY THE RIVER

A SLAB OF HARD ROCK RESISTS BEING WORN AWAY BY THE SEA

WAVES ENTERING A SEA CAVE HAVE WORN A HOLE THROUGH THE ROOF BEYOND

STACKS AND ARCHES ARE FORMED AS SURFACE ROCK IS ERODED BY THE WAVES

WHEN WAVES REACH THE COAST THEY CARVE CLIFFS AND BUILD BEACHES

THE SEABED GRADUALLY RISES FROM THE OCEAN DEPTHS TO THE COAST

Longshore drift
On coasts, waves move sand and shingle along in a zigzag pattern called longshore drift. Groynes (walls or jetties) are sometimes built to slow down this movement, and to build up the quantity of sand on beaches.

Retreating coasts
Given enough time waves will erode (wear down) most coasts (1). Here soft rock is removed, leaving headlands (2). Then these too are eroded away (3).

Frozen Seas

THE EXTREME northern and southern regions of our planet are very cold. The Arctic, in the north, is an ice-covered ocean, surrounded by Greenland and the northern continents. Antarctica, in the south, is a huge continent surrounded by the Southern Ocean.

Glaciers (huge masses of moving ice) have built up to form the ice sheets that cover much of Greenland and Antarctica. In places the ice sheets extend down to the coast and out to sea. Cold winds cause other parts of the sea to freeze, while warmer currents or winds can sometimes melt the sea ice (*see right*).

Few creatures live on the surface of the frozen seas, but near the ice edges there is a rich variety of fish and plankton that provide food for larger animals such as seals and whales.

Melting ice
The amount of ice on Earth varies over time – 25,000 years ago glaciers extended across much of the northern hemisphere. So much water was used up as ice that the sea level was 200 metres lower than it is today.

If all of the ice that rests on land such as Antarctica and Greenland could be melted the sea level would be well over 100 metres higher than it is now, because extra water would be added to the oceans.

RISING WARM WATER MELTS AN AREA OF ICE

ICEBERGS FROM ICE SHEETS CAN BE LARGE ENOUGH TO LAND AN AIRCRAFT ON

RIDGES OF ICE APPEAR WHERE SHEETS OF PACK ICE BUMP INTO EACH OTHER

THE SEA BEGINS TO FREEZE, FORMING PANCAKE ICE – THESE SHEETS GRADUALLY MERGE TOGETHER TO FORM PACK ICE

AN ICEBREAKER BATTERS ITS WAY INTO THE PACK ICE

AT THE BOUNDARY WITH WARMER WATER, THE ICE EDGE THINS OUT AND GRADUALLY DISAPPEARS

UPWELLING OCEAN CURRENTS BRING NUTRIENTS TO FEED PLANKTON (TINY PLANTS AND ANIMALS)

FOR SIX MONTHS OF THE YEAR THE SUN DOES NOT RISE IN THE FAR NORTH OR SOUTH

GLACIERS BUILT UP TO FORM THE VAST ANTARCTIC ICE-SHEET OVER MANY YEARS

AN ICE SHEET CREEPS DOWN-HILL UNDER ITS OWN WEIGHT, AND IS FORMED FROM SNOW AND ICE THAT HAS BUILT UP OVER MANY YEARS

FREEZING WINDS GUST OUT TO SEA FROM THE ICE-BOUND LAND

Seasonal changes

At the poles during the summer, ice melts and daylight returns. In the Arctic, cargo ships can sail along the Siberian coastline. As the ice edge retreats, icebergs drift into the open ocean, gradually melting as they move south. In Antarctica, too, the arrival of the warmer months causes the pack ice to retreat. Migrating birds and animals also move with the seasons, arriving in spring to feast on abundant sea food.

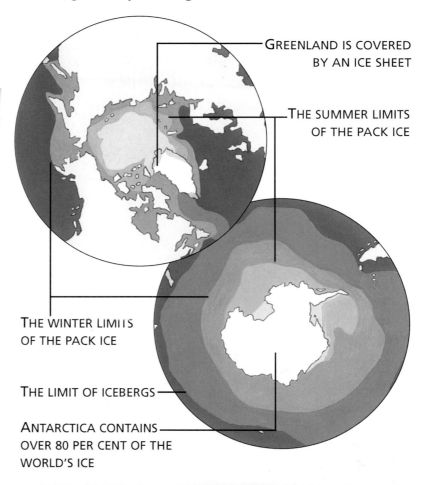

GREENLAND IS COVERED BY AN ICE SHEET

THE SUMMER LIMITS OF THE PACK ICE

THE WINTER LIMITS OF THE PACK ICE

THE LIMIT OF ICEBERGS

ANTARCTICA CONTAINS OVER 80 PER CENT OF THE WORLD'S ICE

ICE SHEETS CAN EXTEND OUT TO SEA FOR SEVERAL KILOMETRES

WHEN SEAWATER FREEZES, SALT IS LEFT BEHIND – THE SALTY WATER SINKS, SETTING UP A CIRCULATION OF WATER

WARM, LESS SALTY WATER FLOWS UP TOWARDS THE SURFACE WHERE IT WILL COOL AND FREEZE, CONTINUING THE CYCLE

ICEBERGS (GIANT LUMPS OF ICE) BREAK AWAY FROM THE ICE EDGE IN A PROCESS CALLED CALVING, THEN DRIFT OUT TO SEA

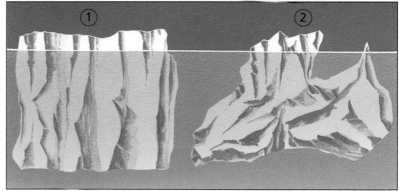

Icebergs

Some icebergs break off immense ice sheets and are as large as an island, taking months or even years to melt (1). They are called 'tabular' (table-like) because of their flat tops. Icebergs that break off glaciers are much smaller (2).

They carry rocky debris, have a more ragged or angular shape, and are mostly found in the Arctic.

Nine-tenths of an iceberg is underneath the water. As it melts, it may become unstable and capsize in a spectacular manner.

Mapping the Sea

TO TAKE measurements at the bottom of the ocean, scientists called oceanographers use sonar (*sound navigation and ranging*) because sound waves travel well in water. They measure depth using a downward-pointing echo sounder, and build up a picture of the ocean floor using a side-scan sonar system. To find out what the ocean floor is made of, columns of earth are pulled up using coring devices. Oceanographers also need to measure the temperature, saltiness, and chemistry of the ocean. They use devices that are lowered or towed from research ships, and take water samples to analyse in the laboratory. Satellites look at sea surface temperature, winds and wave heights, and even plankton cover. Subsurface drifters and pilotless submarines roam the depths, radioing back their findings whenever they surface.

SPECIAL RADAR EQUIPMENT CAN LOOK THROUGH CLOUD TO MEASURE THE OCEAN BELOW

WAVE HEIGHTS CAN BE MEASURED BY SATELLITE ALTIMETERS, WHICH ARE VERY ACCURATE EVEN FROM A HEIGHT OF 800 KILOMETRES

A BATHYSONDE RECORDS TEMPERATURE, SALINITY (SALT CONTENT), AND PRESSURE

THE GIANT PISTON CORER IS USED FOR REMOVING LONG, DEEP SAMPLES OF OCEAN FLOOR

Towed instruments

An undulator is shaped like a small plane, and is towed behind a research ship. It travels down from the surface for 500 metres then travels back up, all the time gathering data such as water temperature. A side-scan sonar is also towed. It gathers data to map the shape of the seabed.

16

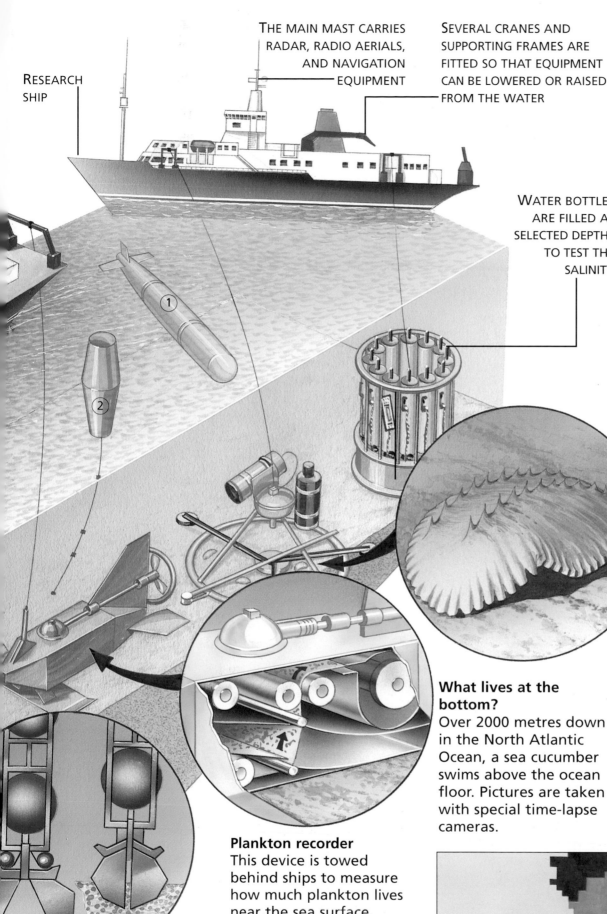

RESEARCH SHIP

THE MAIN MAST CARRIES RADAR, RADIO AERIALS, AND NAVIGATION EQUIPMENT

SEVERAL CRANES AND SUPPORTING FRAMES ARE FITTED SO THAT EQUIPMENT CAN BE LOWERED OR RAISED FROM THE WATER

WATER BOTTLES ARE FILLED AT SELECTED DEPTHS TO TEST THE SALINITY

Research ships
Research ships carry scientists and technicians for several weeks at a time, to gather information about the ocean. Because these ships are extremely expensive to operate there are not that many of them. Robot explorers like the one pictured left (1), are being developed to measure the oceans when ships are not available, or to go on dangerous missions such as exploring under ice caps. Moored buoys (2) are left to measure ocean currents and temperature. They emit radio signals so that they can be found again.

What lives at the bottom?
Over 2000 metres down in the North Atlantic Ocean, a sea cucumber swims above the ocean floor. Pictures are taken with special time-lapse cameras.

Charts and maps
Computers help produce maps of the sea floor by turning sonar images into three-dimensional pictures. Engineers use the maps to plan where to lay cables and pipelines, or to navigate submarines with safety.

Computer models
Information about the ocean is fed into special computer programmes called 'models', which can show how the ocean works. Models can help predict the route of accidental oil spills or how the ocean responds to climate change.

Grab sampler
As its name implies, the grab sampler 'grabs' a sample of the ocean floor and brings it up.

Plankton recorder
This device is towed behind ships to measure how much plankton lives near the sea surface. Seawater and plankton enter through the front and a fine silk mesh inside catches the plankton. The plankton is then stored in a cylinder, ready to be analysed later at a laboratory.

Early Ships

UNTIL THE invention of steam power, the only way ships could move forwards was by using oars or sails. Wind power enabled explorers to travel all over the oceans for hundreds of years, but only in the last hundred years has sail finally given way to other forms of propulsion.

Some of the earliest ships relied on oars – it took many centuries before people learned how to build ships that could move without having the wind behind them. The Vikings and Polynesians rowed for days if the wind was not behind them, and ancient Greeks and Romans relied upon slaves to row their warships and trading ships.

In the 19th century, steam power began to take over from the sail. In ship-building, steel began to replace wood, and in the early 20th century oil began to replace coal as fuel. Steam piston engines were followed by steam turbines, which are still used today by some military vessels and ice-breaking ships, with a nuclear reactor providing the steam.

Developments since steam

Ships like the *Titanic* were built to cross oceans quickly, carrying business-men, immigrants, and mail. After the Second World War, aircraft took over these roles, so large passenger ships were used as cruise liners instead. Steam ships are being retired because, at low speeds, diesel engines are cheaper to run. Gas-turbine (jet-engine) ships were built from the 1970s but they use up a lot of fuel. Today, gas turbines power warships, for which acceleration and speed are important.

Ancient ships

Long-distance voyages were made by the Egyptians in boats built of reeds, palm fibre, and tar. Modern copies have crossed the Atlantic and northern Indian Ocean. Other early ships were built of animal skins and wood, and all of them were used to cross open oceans, though we do not know how many sailors were lost in the attempt.

AN EGYPTIAN REED BOAT, FROM AROUND 2000 BC

SS *GREAT BRITAIN* WAS THE FIRST OCEAN-GOING SHIP TO BE BUILT OF IRON AND THE FIRST PROPELLER-DRIVEN STEAM SHIP TO CROSS THE ATLANTIC

THE CROW'S NEST WHERE LOOKOUTS WATCHED OUT FOR ICEBERGS

A TOTAL OF 1503 PEOPLE DIED WHEN *TITANIC* SANK ON 14 APRIL 1912

TITANIC HAD THREE ENGINES (TWO STEAM PISTON ENGINES AND ONE STEAM TURBINE ENGINE)

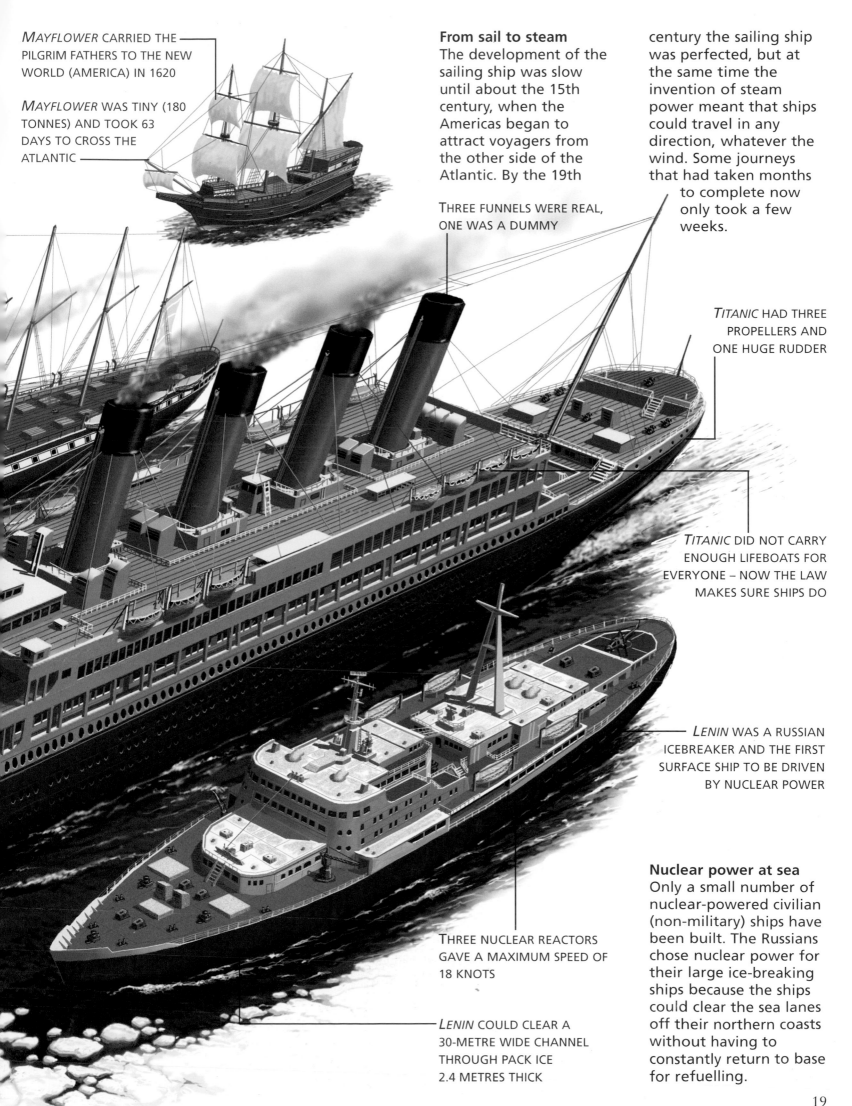

MAYFLOWER CARRIED THE PILGRIM FATHERS TO THE NEW WORLD (AMERICA) IN 1620

MAYFLOWER WAS TINY (180 TONNES) AND TOOK 63 DAYS TO CROSS THE ATLANTIC

From sail to steam

The development of the sailing ship was slow until about the 15th century, when the Americas began to attract voyagers from the other side of the Atlantic. By the 19th century the sailing ship was perfected, but at the same time the invention of steam power meant that ships could travel in any direction, whatever the wind. Some journeys that had taken months to complete now only took a few weeks.

THREE FUNNELS WERE REAL, ONE WAS A DUMMY

TITANIC HAD THREE PROPELLERS AND ONE HUGE RUDDER

TITANIC DID NOT CARRY ENOUGH LIFEBOATS FOR EVERYONE – NOW THE LAW MAKES SURE SHIPS DO

LENIN WAS A RUSSIAN ICEBREAKER AND THE FIRST SURFACE SHIP TO BE DRIVEN BY NUCLEAR POWER

THREE NUCLEAR REACTORS GAVE A MAXIMUM SPEED OF 18 KNOTS

Nuclear power at sea

Only a small number of nuclear-powered civilian (non-military) ships have been built. The Russians chose nuclear power for their large ice-breaking ships because the ships could clear the sea lanes off their northern coasts without having to constantly return to base for refuelling.

LENIN COULD CLEAR A 30-METRE WIDE CHANNEL THROUGH PACK ICE 2.4 METRES THICK

Modern Ships

MOST MODERN ships are built of steel and powered by diesel engines. They are usually equipped with a lot of automated machinery so that only a small crew is needed. Satellites and computers control navigation, backed up with traditional instruments such as the sextant.

Running ships cheaply is now more important than travelling at top speed, except for specialist ships such as express ferries, which commonly use twin-hull designs. In the future there will be more ships using two or three small, streamlined hulls as they give high speed without needing a lot of expensive fuel. Their narrow, smooth shapes cut more easily through the water. Any water resistance can slow a ship down, so a streamlined shape helps a ship to go faster.

Luxury cruise liner
Ocean liners no longer carry passengers travelling from one port to another. Today, people take their holidays on board ocean liners. Instead of high speed, comfort has become the priority, so the ships have smooth-running diesel engines, stabilizers to help keep the ship steady, and full air-conditioning.

Why do ships float?
The metal hull of a ship encloses a vast amount of air. This means a cubic metre of ship weighs much less than a cubic metre of water, so a ship floats. If the hull was solid metal the ship would sink like a stone.

THE FUNNEL OR STACK CARRIES EXHAUSTS AND AIR INTAKES FOR THE MAIN ENGINES

THERE ARE MANY SWIMMING POOLS, INDOOR AND OUTDOOR, ON BOARD

SATELLITE COMMUNICATIONS EQUIPMENT PROVIDES CONSTANT CONTACT WITH THE MAINLAND

CASINOS, SHOPPING MALLS, AND HAIRDRESSERS ARE ALL AVAILABLE ON BOARD

PASSENGERS RELAX ON THE AFT DECK

ROPES CAN BE USED TO HELP THE SHIP TO DOCK

TWIN RUDDERS STEER THE SHIP – CROSS WINDS CAN EASILY BLOW SUCH A HIGH-SIDED SHIP OFF COURSE

LIFEBOATS AND RAFTS ARE CARRIED SO PASSENGERS CAN ESCAPE IN EMERGENCIES

Stabilizers

Most passenger ships use stabilizers to reduce roll (*see left*). These are often in the form of fins, like small wings. They use gyroscopes, computer software, and hydraulic jacks to react quickly to the ship's roll, and provide lift or down-force so the ship is kept on an even keel. When the sea is calm, they are retracted to prevent damage.

Propeller design

Great care goes into the design and manufacture of propellers. If just one blade is out of balance the smooth propulsion of a ship can be ruined. Modern designs use several curved blades, and on some ships the blades can be rotated to provide reverse thrust.

THE MOST EXPENSIVE CABINS ARE HIGH UP

THE BRIDGE HOUSES THE SHIP'S MAIN CONTROLS

THE FORWARD WEATHER DECK CAN WITHSTAND HEAVY WAVES

NAVIGATION, RADIO, AND RADAR EQUIPMENT ARE CARRIED ON THE MAIN MAST

THE FORWARD AUDITORIUM IS A FULL-SIZE THEATRE

A BOW THRUSTER HELPS THE SHIP TURN

STABILIZER FINS ENSURE A COMFORTABLE CRUISE

HEAVY EQUIPMENT, FUEL, AND STORES IN THE LOWEST PART OF THE SHIP AID STABILITY

ELECTRIC MOTORS TURN THE PROPELLER SHAFTS

POWERFUL DIESEL ENGINES TURN GENERATORS TO PROVIDE ELECTRICITY FOR ALL THE SHIP'S NEEDS

Satellite navigation

Global Positioning System (GPS) satellites carry highly accurate atomic clocks and send time and position data to GPS receivers fitted to ships and aircraft. The receiver compares signals from two or more satellites and can work out its position to within a few metres. Buoys fitted with radio beacons also help to confirm a ship's position.

Fishing

ACROSS THE WORLD there is a high demand for fish and squid, so there are always large fleets of fishing vessels on the ocean. Because the demand for fish is so high, nations are able to monitor and control fishing up to 200 nautical miles from their coasts. Governments use aircraft or satellites to watch out for illegal fishing. Inspectors can go aboard fishing vessels to check that regulations are being followed.

A fishing crew lives and works aboard ship 24 hours a day and is often paid according to the value of the catch. Even today, deep-sea fishing remains a tiring and physically dangerous job.

Factory ship

Fishing grounds can be a long way from the country where the fish will be eaten. Some ships are equipped like factories so they can turn fish into products that can be sold at the end of the voyage, perhaps several months' journey away. On board the fish are gutted and the quality fish fillets are sorted and deep frozen. The organs are stored or processed into fish oils and chemicals, and the offcuts, heads, and bones turned into fishmeal, pastes, and cheaper foods. Nothing is wasted, and the ship will stay at sea until the hold is full or fuel runs low.

THE A-FRAME HOLDS THE NET AND CABLES CLEAR OF OBSTRUCTIONS ON THE STERN

WINCHES (REELS) ARE COMPUTER CONTROLLED TO KEEP THE NET AT THE RIGHT DEPTH

AS THE CATCH ARRIVES, THE CREW SET TO WORK – GUTTING AND PROCESSING

THE CREW CAN HARNESS THEMSELVES TO RAILS SO THAT THEY ARE NOT SWEPT OVERBOARD IN ROUGH SEAS

CRANES ARE USED TO HANDLE THE CABLES AND NETS

THE NET IS HAULED BACK ON BOARD UP THE SLOPING STERN RAMP

A POWERFUL PROPELLER AND DOUBLE-HINGED RUDDER MAKE THE SHIP EASIER TO MANOEUVRE

THE MAIN DIESEL ENGINE IS HEAVY AND SITS DEEP IN THE HULL, HELPING STABILITY

THE ENGINE ROOM PROVIDES POWER FOR WINCHES AND THE SHIP'S ELECTRICAL SUPPLY

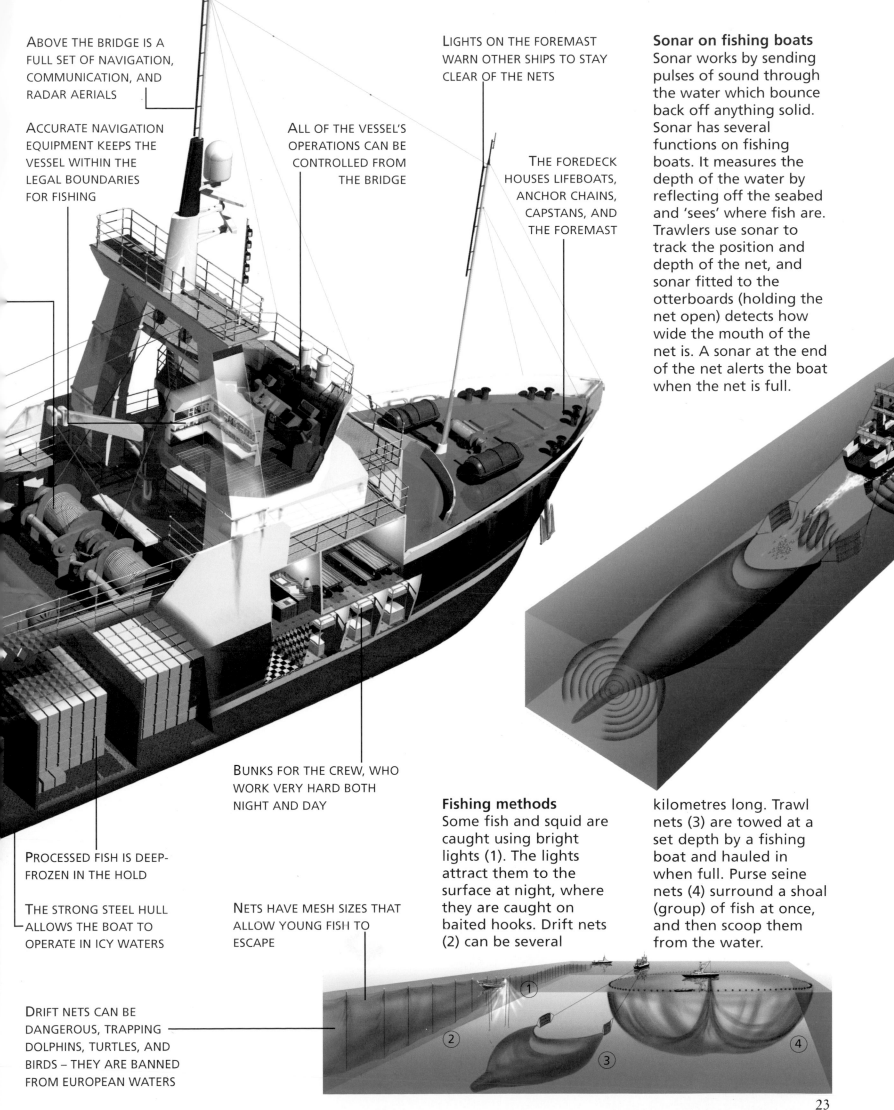

ABOVE THE BRIDGE IS A FULL SET OF NAVIGATION, COMMUNICATION, AND RADAR AERIALS

ACCURATE NAVIGATION EQUIPMENT KEEPS THE VESSEL WITHIN THE LEGAL BOUNDARIES FOR FISHING

ALL OF THE VESSEL'S OPERATIONS CAN BE CONTROLLED FROM THE BRIDGE

LIGHTS ON THE FOREMAST WARN OTHER SHIPS TO STAY CLEAR OF THE NETS

THE FOREDECK HOUSES LIFEBOATS, ANCHOR CHAINS, CAPSTANS, AND THE FOREMAST

Sonar on fishing boats
Sonar works by sending pulses of sound through the water which bounce back off anything solid. Sonar has several functions on fishing boats. It measures the depth of the water by reflecting off the seabed and 'sees' where fish are. Trawlers use sonar to track the position and depth of the net, and sonar fitted to the otterboards (holding the net open) detects how wide the mouth of the net is. A sonar at the end of the net alerts the boat when the net is full.

BUNKS FOR THE CREW, WHO WORK VERY HARD BOTH NIGHT AND DAY

PROCESSED FISH IS DEEP-FROZEN IN THE HOLD

THE STRONG STEEL HULL ALLOWS THE BOAT TO OPERATE IN ICY WATERS

NETS HAVE MESH SIZES THAT ALLOW YOUNG FISH TO ESCAPE

Fishing methods
Some fish and squid are caught using bright lights (1). The lights attract them to the surface at night, where they are caught on baited hooks. Drift nets (2) can be several

kilometres long. Trawl nets (3) are towed at a set depth by a fishing boat and hauled in when full. Purse seine nets (4) surround a shoal (group) of fish at once, and then scoop them from the water.

DRIFT NETS CAN BE DANGEROUS, TRAPPING DOLPHINS, TURTLES, AND BIRDS – THEY ARE BANNED FROM EUROPEAN WATERS

Submarines

THERE ARE many submarines operating in the world's oceans. A few are small, carrying just two or three people. They are used by people doing scientific research or construction work, and stay underwater for only a few hours at a time.

Military submarines are much larger. There are three basic types: missile-carrying (*right*), hunter-killer, and diesel-electric. The main reason why missiles are carried by submarines is that submarines are hidden underwater and are hard for the enemy to find. However, the hunter-killer submarine is designed to find and destroy the missile-carrying submarines of enemies as well as the enemies' own hunter-killer submarines. The diesel-electric submarine is the quietest type. It is used for missions where stealth is important, such as secretly landing soldiers near an enemy coast.

Ballistic-missile submarine

Some countries use massive ballistic-missile submarines, which carry nuclear weapons. The submarines remain deep under the ocean or under ice caps for several months at a time. The idea behind them is known as 'deterrence': if a country was ever attacked and destroyed by a nuclear weapon, its submarines would survive to launch a revenge attack on the enemy country. The belief is that if an enemy country knows this threat of revenge exists, they will be deterred (put off) from launching an attack in the first place.

Staying hidden

The most important thing for military submarines is to avoid being found, so they rarely surface, raise periscopes, or use radio to speak to base. Because sound carries easily underwater, submarines are built to be as quiet as possible. Mechanics are taught to be careful not to drop their tools, and if necessary the submarine will sit motionless for days. However, it is impossible to be completely silent, and trailing hunter-killer submarines will listen out for the slightest hint that there might be a target nearby.

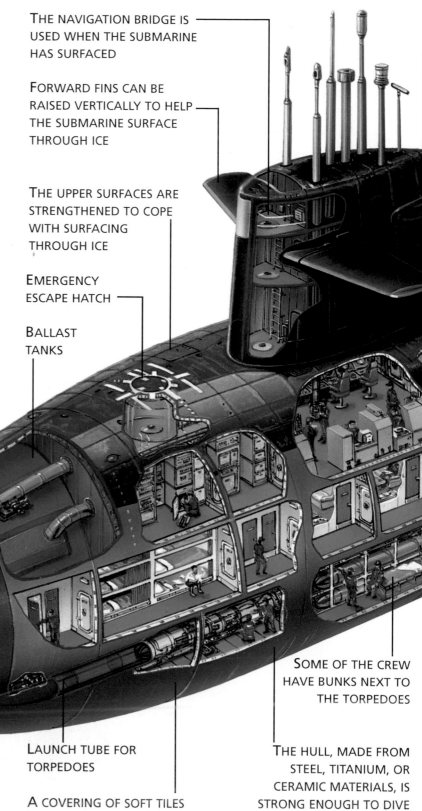

THE NAVIGATION BRIDGE IS USED WHEN THE SUBMARINE HAS SURFACED

FORWARD FINS CAN BE RAISED VERTICALLY TO HELP THE SUBMARINE SURFACE THROUGH ICE

THE UPPER SURFACES ARE STRENGTHENED TO COPE WITH SURFACING THROUGH ICE

EMERGENCY ESCAPE HATCH

BALLAST TANKS

THE STREAMLINED NOSE AIDS SPEED AND REDUCES NOISE

INSIDE THE NOSE IS THE SONAR DOME WHICH EMITS SOUNDS TO DETECT OTHER SOLID OBJECTS IN THE SEA

LAUNCH TUBE FOR TORPEDOES

A COVERING OF SOFT TILES ABSORBS SOUND

SOME OF THE CREW HAVE BUNKS NEXT TO THE TORPEDOES

THE HULL, MADE FROM STEEL, TITANIUM, OR CERAMIC MATERIALS, IS STRONG ENOUGH TO DIVE OVER 600 METRES

Detection by sound

A submarine uses sonar (sound navigation and ranging) to detect solid objects. Sonar can be active, where the submarine emits sounds which are reflected back from the target, or passive, where the submarine just listens to the noises that other vessels or large animals are making.

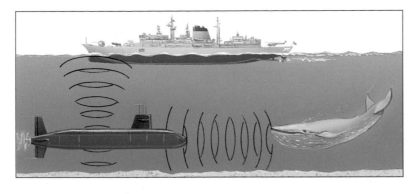

THIS TOWER CARRIES THE RADAR, PERISCOPES, AND COMMUNICATIONS EQUIPMENT

MISSILE HATCHES

THE MISSILE IS LAUNCHED FROM THE TUBE WITH A PUFF OF GAS – ITS ROCKET ENGINE LIGHTS AS IT REACHES THE SURFACE

EACH MISSILE CARRIES SEVERAL NUCLEAR WARHEADS

THE NUCLEAR REACTOR CAN OPERATE FOR SEVERAL YEARS WITHOUT REFUELLING

LARGE RUDDERS KEEP THE SUBMARINE STEADY

THE PROPELLER IS DESIGNED TO MAKE LITTLE NOISE AND NO BUBBLES

BALLAST TANKS

EMERGENCY BATTERIES IN CASE OF MAIN POWER FAILURE

MISSILES HAVE SOLID-FUEL ROCKET ENGINES

THE MISSILES ARE CARRIED IN TUBES – THEY CAN BE LAUNCHED WHILE THE SUBMARINE IS UNDERWATER

STEAM IS GENERATED AS WATER PASSES THROUGH THE REACTOR, AND IT DRIVES A TURBINE

THE TURBINE GENERATES ELECTRICITY FOR THE MAIN MOTOR AND ALL THE SUBMARINE'S SYSTEMS

Diving and surfacing

In order to sink, a submarine has to become heavier. It does this by filling large tanks, called ballast tanks, with seawater (1). If it has to surface, compressed air is blown back into the ballast tanks to push out the water (2). This makes the submarine lighter again, and more buoyant (able to float). Some submarines have been lost at sea when something has gone wrong with the ballast tank system.

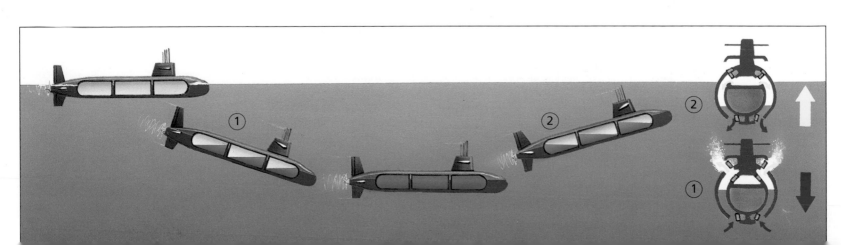

Scuba Diving

SCUBA (self-contained underwater breathing apparatus) has enabled people to explore the ocean to a depth of about 30 metres, and deeper, using special air mixtures. At greater depths the water pressure has dangerous effects on the diver (the water pressure increases with depth).

Pioneers like Jacques Cousteau and Hans Hass made scuba diving very popular, and today people dive all over the world. In fact diving is so popular that it has become a problem in some places because too many divers can damage fragile corals and affect the normal behaviour of fish.

Although diving is quite safe, training is essential. Divers learn safety drills and calculate how long they have been at depth, so that they can surface without getting the bends, a painful condition where air bubbles form inside the body.

Breathing apparatus
The tank strapped to the diver's back contains air for the diver to breathe. At the top of the air tank, level with the diver's lungs, is a valve called a regulator. Air passes through the regulator down a tube to the mouthpiece. The regulator reduces the pressure of the air that comes out of the tank. The pressure is further reduced by the demand valve in the mouthpiece. This ensures the air

THE REGULATOR CONTROLS THE FLOW OF AIR FROM THE AIR TANK AND REDUCES THE AIR'S PRESSURE

PIPE TO THE MOUTHPIECE

THE FACE MASK ENABLES THE DIVER TO SEE UNDERWATER

FLASH UNIT FOR CAMERA

ELECTRICAL ITEMS MUST BE WATERPROOF

AIR TUBE TO THE BC JACKET

FLOW OF EXHAUST AIR WHEN BREATHING OUT

UNDERWATER PHOTOGRAPHY IS OF GREAT INTEREST TO MANY SPORTS DIVERS

DEMAND VALVE

DIVER BREATHES THROUGH VALVE

A DIAPHRAGM IN THE VALVE EQUALIZES AIR AND WATER PRESSURE

breathed is at the same pressure as that of the water around. Divers must breathe smoothly all the time and not hold their breath, because as they travel up to the surface, air expands and could burst their lungs!

THE AIR TANK CARRIES HIGHLY COMPRESSED (SQUEEZED) AIR MIXTURES

DIVERS MUST TAKE CARE NOT TO DAMAGE CORALS WITH THEIR FINS

SWIM FINS ARE USED TO PROPEL THE DIVER

NEOPRENE WET SUIT, HAT, GLOVES, AND SOCKS KEEP THE COLD OUT

DIVERS WEAR A KNIFE TO USE IF THEY GET TANGLED UP IN NETS, LINES, OR SEAWEEDS

THE WETSUIT'S BRIGHT COLOURS MAKE THE DIVER EASIER TO SEE

A BC (BUOYANCY COMPENSATOR) IS A JACKET THAT CAN BE INFLATED WITH AIR TO HELP THE DIVER RISE TO THE SURFACE

WEIGHT BELT SO THAT THE DIVER CAN SINK EASILY

COMPASS, AND GAUGES THAT SHOW DEPTH AND AMOUNT OF AIR LEFT IN TANK

THE COMPASS IS ESSENTIAL IN MURKY WATERS

MANY DIVERS USE A DIVE COMPUTER TO KEEP TRACK OF TIME AND CALCULATE THE SPEED AT WHICH THEY ARE RISING TO THE SURFACE

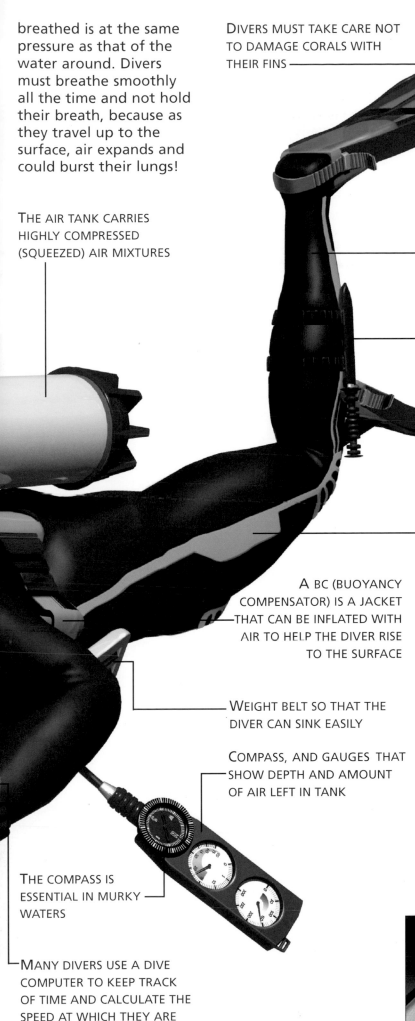

'OK' – EVERYTHING IS ALL RIGHT ON THE SURFACE

'NOT OK' – HELP NEEDED ON THE SURFACE

'ARE YOU OK?'/'I AM OKAY'

'HELP!'

Wetsuits
In a wetsuit a layer of neoprene foam rubber insulates against cold, and can be bought in various thicknesses depending upon water temperature. The wetsuit is designed so that water leaks into it through the neck, leg, and armholes. The body then warms up the thin layer of water between the wetsuit and skin, keeping the diver warm for hours.

Hand signals
Although there are gadgets that enable you to speak underwater, most divers don't have them so they rely on hand signals. There is an international code of hand signals so that divers can work safely anywhere in the world. Divers never dive alone. They always have a fellow diver to keep an eye on them and watch out for distress signals.

Submersibles

SUBMERSIBLES are small, deep-diving vehicles that were first used in the search for wreckage of lost aircraft, ships, and weapons. Today, they are most often used by scientists exploring mysterious features of the deep ocean floor, such as trenches and volcanic ridges. Compared with military submarines, submersibles cannot stay under the surface of the water for very long – usually a few hours, or a day or two at the most. However, they are more useful to scientists. They can dive far deeper than any military submarine, some to 6000 metres or more. They also have windows, camera systems, and mechanical hands so that the crew can view and handle things at the bottom of the sea.

Today, rigid diving suits can almost do the same job as submersibles and some, such as the *Newt* suit, use small propellers to move about.

Trieste

Trieste 1 was designed to reach the greatest depths possible. On 23 January 1960 she carried Jacques Piccard and Don Walsh to a record depth of 10,912 metres at the bottom of a gorge in the Pacific Ocean.

Trieste had two ballast tanks filled with heavy iron shot. To surface, the iron shot was released, making *Trieste* lighter and able to rise. A large tank filled with petrol gave buoyancy. The crew sat below in a steel sphere.

UNDERWATER TELEPHONE TRANSMITTER

THE TOWER IS BRIGHTLY COLOURED SO THAT IT CAN BE EASILY SEEN WHEN THE CRAFT HAS SURFACED

THE SONAR SCANNER CAN FIND HIDDEN OBSTACLES

TV CAMERAS RECORD EVERYTHING GOING ON OUTSIDE. PLENTY OF LIGHTS PENETRATE THE DARKNESS

THE CABIN IS LIKE A METAL BALL

MECHANICAL ARMS COLLECT OBJECTS FROM THE OCEAN FLOOR

A LARGE TANK, CALLED THE FLOAT, PROVIDED BUOYANCY

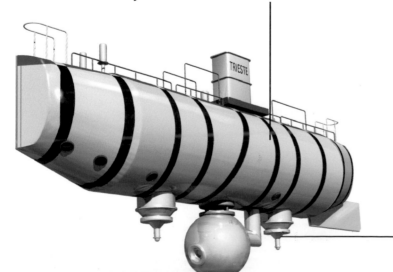

WITH THE HELP OF LASER TECHNOLOGY, ARM CONTROL IS PRECISE

TWO TANKS CONTAINED METAL BALLAST

A COLLECTING CAGE CARRIES SAMPLE BOTTLES, ROCK SPECIMENS, AND ITEMS FROM SHIPWRECKS

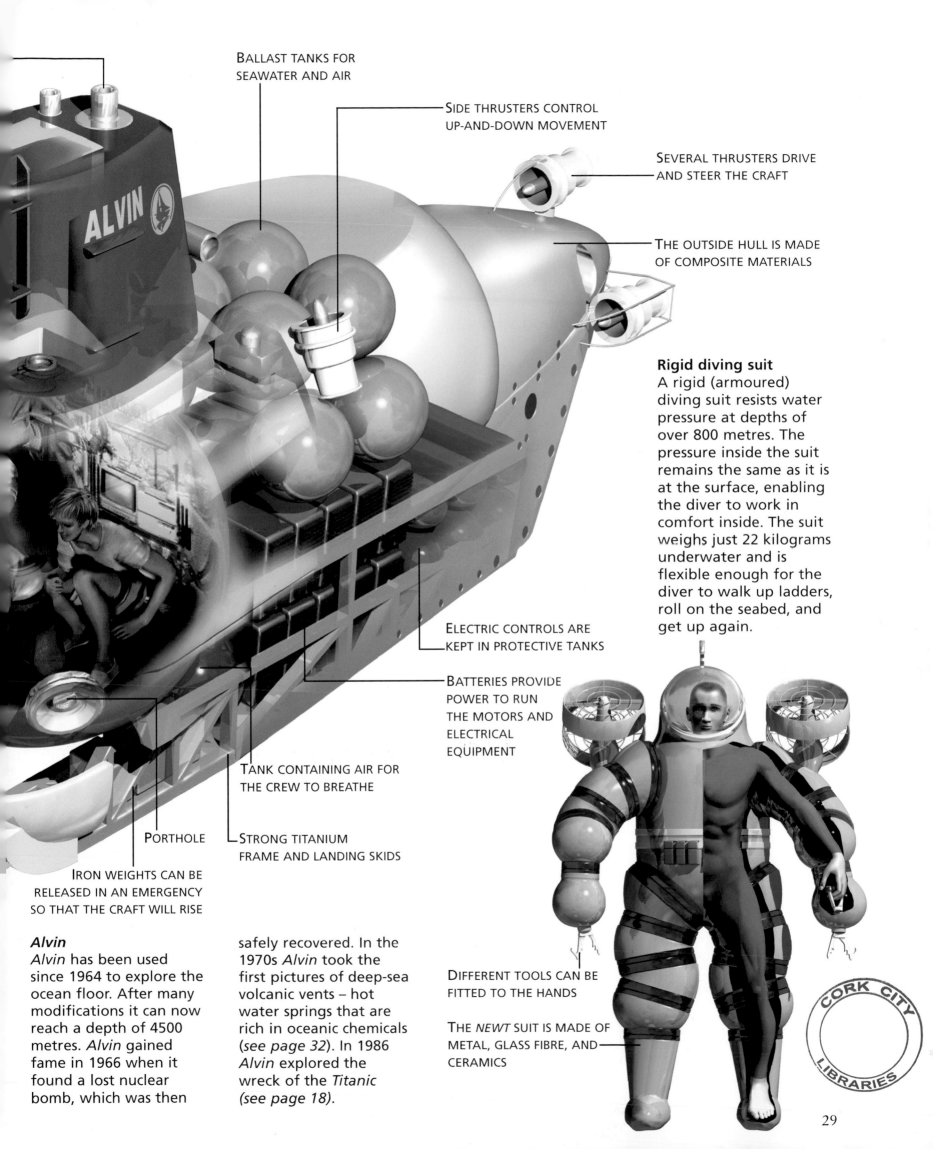

BALLAST TANKS FOR
SEAWATER AND AIR

SIDE THRUSTERS CONTROL
UP-AND-DOWN MOVEMENT

SEVERAL THRUSTERS DRIVE
AND STEER THE CRAFT

ALVIN

THE OUTSIDE HULL IS MADE
OF COMPOSITE MATERIALS

Rigid diving suit
A rigid (armoured)
diving suit resists water
pressure at depths of
over 800 metres. The
pressure inside the suit
remains the same as it is
at the surface, enabling
the diver to work in
comfort inside. The suit
weighs just 22 kilograms
underwater and is
flexible enough for the
diver to walk up ladders,
roll on the seabed, and
get up again.

ELECTRIC CONTROLS ARE
KEPT IN PROTECTIVE TANKS

BATTERIES PROVIDE
POWER TO RUN
THE MOTORS AND
ELECTRICAL
EQUIPMENT

TANK CONTAINING AIR FOR
THE CREW TO BREATHE

PORTHOLE

STRONG TITANIUM
FRAME AND LANDING SKIDS

IRON WEIGHTS CAN BE
RELEASED IN AN EMERGENCY
SO THAT THE CRAFT WILL RISE

DIFFERENT TOOLS CAN BE
FITTED TO THE HANDS

THE *NEWT* SUIT IS MADE OF
METAL, GLASS FIBRE, AND
CERAMICS

Alvin
Alvin has been used
since 1964 to explore the
ocean floor. After many
modifications it can now
reach a depth of 4500
metres. *Alvin* gained
fame in 1966 when it
found a lost nuclear
bomb, which was then

safely recovered. In the
1970s *Alvin* took the
first pictures of deep-sea
volcanic vents – hot
water springs that are
rich in oceanic chemicals
(*see page 32*). In 1986
Alvin explored the
wreck of the *Titanic*
(*see page 18*).

29

Shipwrecks

IN AN average year about 150 ships sink because of accidents, severe storms, and, most commonly, human error. Some of these wrecks cause major pollution problems, but the ocean's natural forces are able to cope with most types of waste. Iron-eating bacteria start working on the hull, worms eat up the wood, and chemical action sorts out what is left. After a few hundred years a lot of the shipwreck has gone, leaving behind fewer clues for explorers.

As diving technology has advanced, getting valuable items from shipwrecks has become easier. At first, only recovering treasure and cannons was considered worth the risk involved. Later it became possible to raise the wrecks by patching up holes and pumping in air.

The development of deep-ocean exploration systems was encouraged by the need to find missing submarines and nuclear weapons during the Cold War years. It has resulted in spectacular findings including Dr Bob Ballard's discovery of the *Titanic* and *Bismarck*.

Wreck hunting

Finding deep wrecks is not easy because the ocean is so big. First there is a survey of the area where the wreck might be, using side-scan sonar and cameras mounted on sledges. When the wreck is found, detailed exploration can begin using TV cameras attached to remote-operated vehicles (ROVs). A submersible like *Alvin* may be used so the explorers can examine the wreck close-up.

Viewing the remains

An ROV camera travels inside the wreck to bring back images of familiar objects. There are no dead bodies – they were eaten long ago by fish.

What a side-scan sees

A side-scan sonar gives a one-colour image of shadows. Computers help to improve the picture quality, but recognizing what the image shows still requires skill and experience.

THE CREW WORK IN A TITANIUM SPHERE WITH THICK WINDOWS – WATER PRESSURE AT 3000 METRES IS 300 TIMES GREATER THAN ATMOSPHERIC PRESSURE

THE SUBMERSIBLE'S PROPELLER IS PROTECTED BY A LIGHT COVERING SO THAT PIECES OF RIGGING, WIRE, OR ROPE WILL NOT TRAP THE VESSEL ON THE SEA FLOOR

A REMOTE MANIPULATOR ARM LIFTS ITEMS FROM THE OCEAN FLOOR – SOME PIECES MAY BE BROUGHT TO THE SURFACE FOR CLOSER EXAMINATION

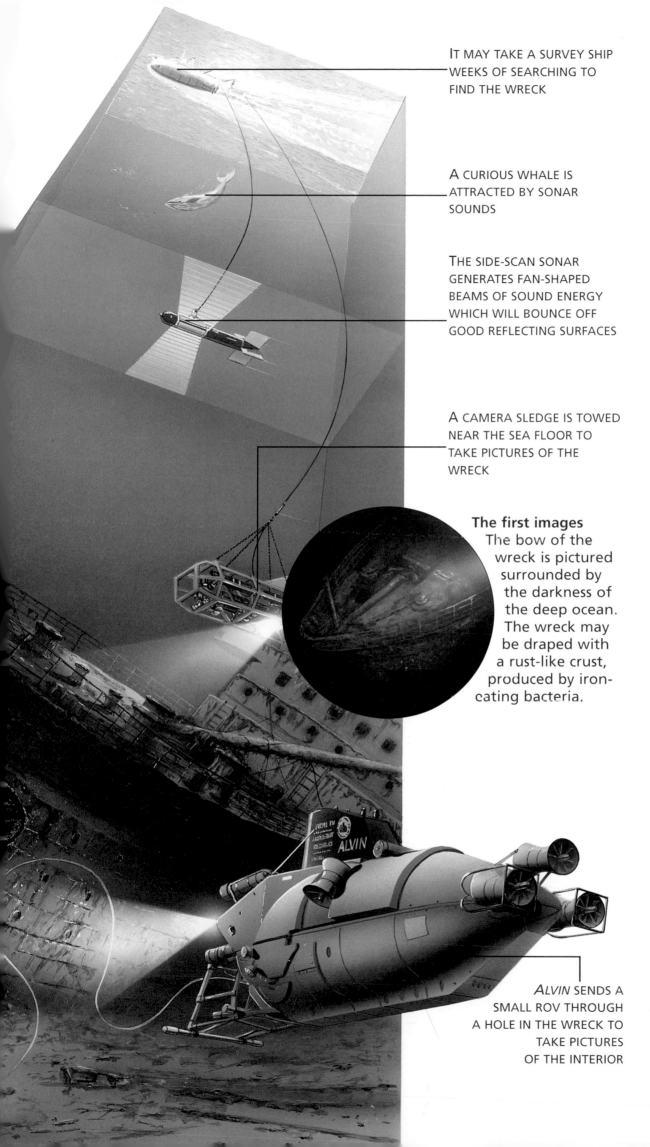

IT MAY TAKE A SURVEY SHIP WEEKS OF SEARCHING TO FIND THE WRECK

A CURIOUS WHALE IS ATTRACTED BY SONAR SOUNDS

THE SIDE-SCAN SONAR GENERATES FAN-SHAPED BEAMS OF SOUND ENERGY WHICH WILL BOUNCE OFF GOOD REFLECTING SURFACES

A CAMERA SLEDGE IS TOWED NEAR THE SEA FLOOR TO TAKE PICTURES OF THE WRECK

The first images

The bow of the wreck is pictured surrounded by the darkness of the deep ocean. The wreck may be draped with a rust-like crust, produced by iron-eating bacteria.

ALVIN SENDS A SMALL ROV THROUGH A HOLE IN THE WRECK TO TAKE PICTURES OF THE INTERIOR

Looking for ancient wrecks

In the warm, clear waters of the Mediterranean, marine archaeologists hunt for the wrecks of ancient Greek, Roman, and Persian ships. The wooden parts will have been eaten away unless well buried, but metal remains can be found by a submersible metal detector.

A diver photographs the cargo of a Roman shipwreck. A survey grid enables the position of items to be accurately recorded.

A cannon is raised using lifting bags that were filled with air at the seabed. The diver releases air pressure to control ascent speed. Larger bags can raise aircraft, ships, and submarines.

Ocean Life

THE OCEANS teem with a wide variety of life, from tiny bacteria to huge whales. Scientists believe that life on earth first began in the oceans. Today, land animals still have salty blood – perhaps this is a sign of their ancient connection to the oceans.

Life exists throughout the ocean, even in the deepest, darkest trenches of the ocean floor and in icy polar waters. At the surface, phytoplankton (tiny floating plants) use the energy of the Sun to make food. Animals graze on the plankton, and are in turn eaten by larger hunters and scavengers. In very deep water where there is no light for plants to grow, and in the thick mud of the ocean floor, worms, bacteria, and other creatures feed on the material that has sunk all the way down from above.

There is one very unusual group of creatures on the ocean floor which feed on chemicals rather than animal or plant matter. They live near hot water springs.

Something for everyone
In the ocean, every possible niche (living space) is taken up by one or more life form. New creatures are constantly being discovered as researchers learn more about the deep oceans. Scientists were amazed to discover that life could exist around deep-sea hot water vents. From these volcanic vents water gushes up at temperatures of 400°C carrying a dissolved mixture of strong chemicals. The source of energy for most animals stems from the Sun: animals eat plants which use sunlight to make their food energy. But the creatures living near the volcanic vents get their energy from eating bacteria which change the chemicals they have absorbed into energy.

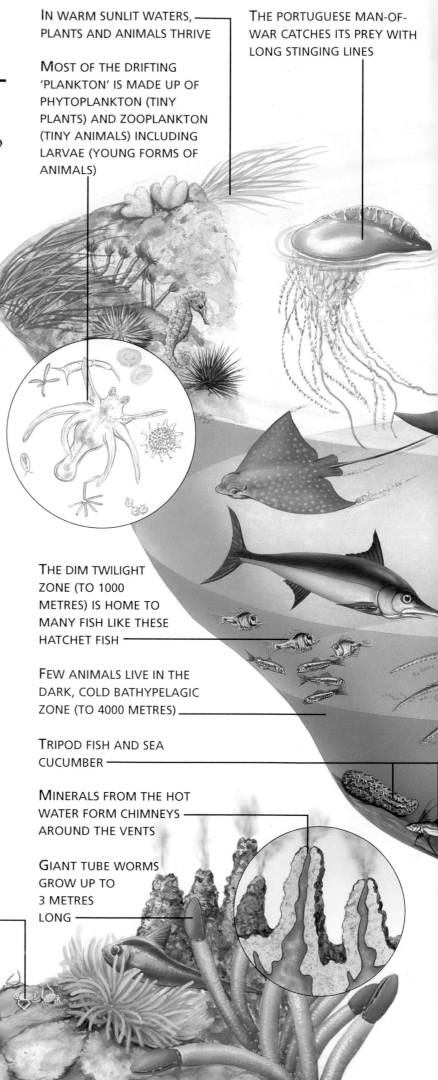

IN WARM SUNLIT WATERS, PLANTS AND ANIMALS THRIVE

THE PORTUGUESE MAN-OF-WAR CATCHES ITS PREY WITH LONG STINGING LINES

MOST OF THE DRIFTING 'PLANKTON' IS MADE UP OF PHYTOPLANKTON (TINY PLANTS) AND ZOOPLANKTON (TINY ANIMALS) INCLUDING LARVAE (YOUNG FORMS OF ANIMALS)

THE DIM TWILIGHT ZONE (TO 1000 METRES) IS HOME TO MANY FISH LIKE THESE HATCHET FISH

FEW ANIMALS LIVE IN THE DARK, COLD BATHYPELAGIC ZONE (TO 4000 METRES)

TRIPOD FISH AND SEA CUCUMBER

MINERALS FROM THE HOT WATER FORM CHIMNEYS AROUND THE VENTS

GIANT TUBE WORMS GROW UP TO 3 METRES LONG

DEEP-SEA CRABS AND FISH THRIVE NEAR A HOT WATER VENT

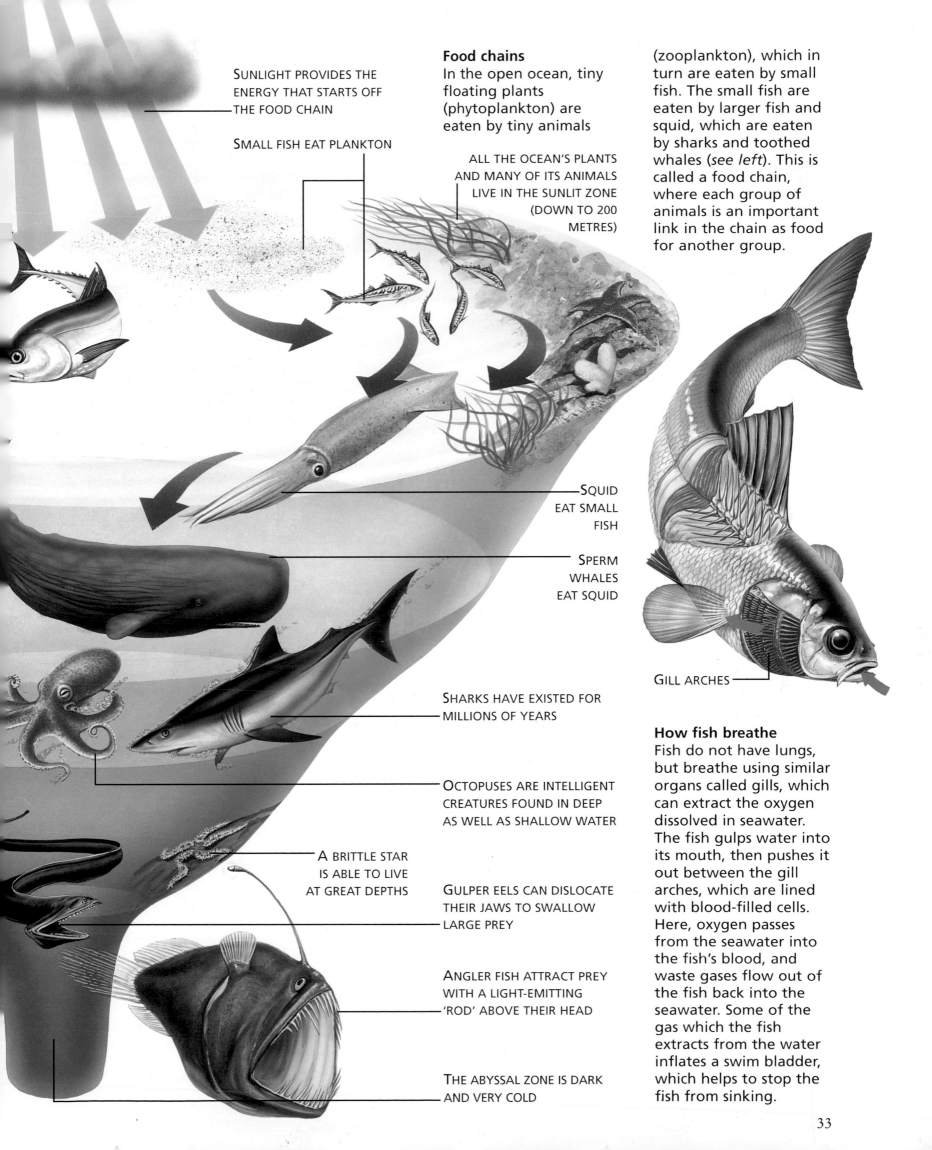

SUNLIGHT PROVIDES THE ENERGY THAT STARTS OFF THE FOOD CHAIN

SMALL FISH EAT PLANKTON

Food chains
In the open ocean, tiny floating plants (phytoplankton) are eaten by tiny animals

ALL THE OCEAN'S PLANTS AND MANY OF ITS ANIMALS LIVE IN THE SUNLIT ZONE (DOWN TO 200 METRES)

(zooplankton), which in turn are eaten by small fish. The small fish are eaten by larger fish and squid, which are eaten by sharks and toothed whales (*see left*). This is called a food chain, where each group of animals is an important link in the chain as food for another group.

SQUID EAT SMALL FISH

SPERM WHALES EAT SQUID

SHARKS HAVE EXISTED FOR MILLIONS OF YEARS

OCTOPUSES ARE INTELLIGENT CREATURES FOUND IN DEEP AS WELL AS SHALLOW WATER

A BRITTLE STAR IS ABLE TO LIVE AT GREAT DEPTHS

GULPER EELS CAN DISLOCATE THEIR JAWS TO SWALLOW LARGE PREY

ANGLER FISH ATTRACT PREY WITH A LIGHT-EMITTING 'ROD' ABOVE THEIR HEAD

THE ABYSSAL ZONE IS DARK AND VERY COLD

GILL ARCHES

How fish breathe
Fish do not have lungs, but breathe using similar organs called gills, which can extract the oxygen dissolved in seawater. The fish gulps water into its mouth, then pushes it out between the gill arches, which are lined with blood-filled cells. Here, oxygen passes from the seawater into the fish's blood, and waste gases flow out of the fish back into the seawater. Some of the gas which the fish extracts from the water inflates a swim bladder, which helps to stop the fish from sinking.

Coastal Life

ANIMALS AND plants that live on the coast need to be hardy and adaptable as they have to cope with periods in and out of the water as the tides change the sea level. Some seaweeds produce slime to help stop them from drying out at low tide. Many animals burrow into the wet sand, hide under seaweed, or close up their shells while the tide is out. Coastal plants and animals in exposed places also need to be strong enough to stand up to the waves, and be able to put up with changes in the saltiness of the water when it rains.

A much greater variety of animals and plants live in rockpools, where they do not suffer from drying out as the tide goes down. But they still have to cope with large changes in temperature as the pool warms up in the sun or cools down in winter, and with freshwater when it rains.

Coastal life zones

The splash zone lies above high tide but is regularly sprayed with salt water. It's a hard place to live, and few species are seen here. Typical ones are yellow, orange and black lichens, and snails.

The intertidal zone, between high and low tide, is home to creatures such as barnacles, limpets, mussels, sea anemones, and crabs. Plants include brown, green, and red seaweed.

Below low-tide level live many more kinds of plants and animals. In colder waters, great forests of large brown seaweeds, called kelp, live on rocks, sheltering delicate red seaweeds, fish, and many other animals, while in warm waters coral reefs thrive.

Burrowing on the beach

In the sand many animals burrow with skill. With its hind flippers, the female loggerhead turtle digs a hole in which to lay her eggs (1). Razors (2) have a long shell – a powerful 'foot' at the bottom helps them to move up or down. The sand gaper (3) has an oval shell and feeds through two tubes that stretch up to the surface. Sea potatoes (4) are burrowing sea urchins. The sea mouse (5) is actually a worm covered in fine hairs. Lugworms (6) swallow sand to feed, passing out what's left as a worm cast.

SEAWEEDS SECURELY ATTACH THEMSELVES TO ROCKS

SAND, GRAVEL, MUD, AND ROCK FORM THE SEABED

THE LEAVES OF THIS GIANT KELP STRETCH UP TOWARDS THE SURFACE WATERS TO RECEIVE SUNLIGHT

SEAWEEDS CLING FIRMLY TO ROCKS SO THAT THEY ARE NOT SWEPT OUT TO SEA

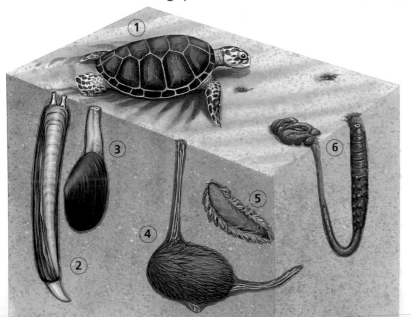

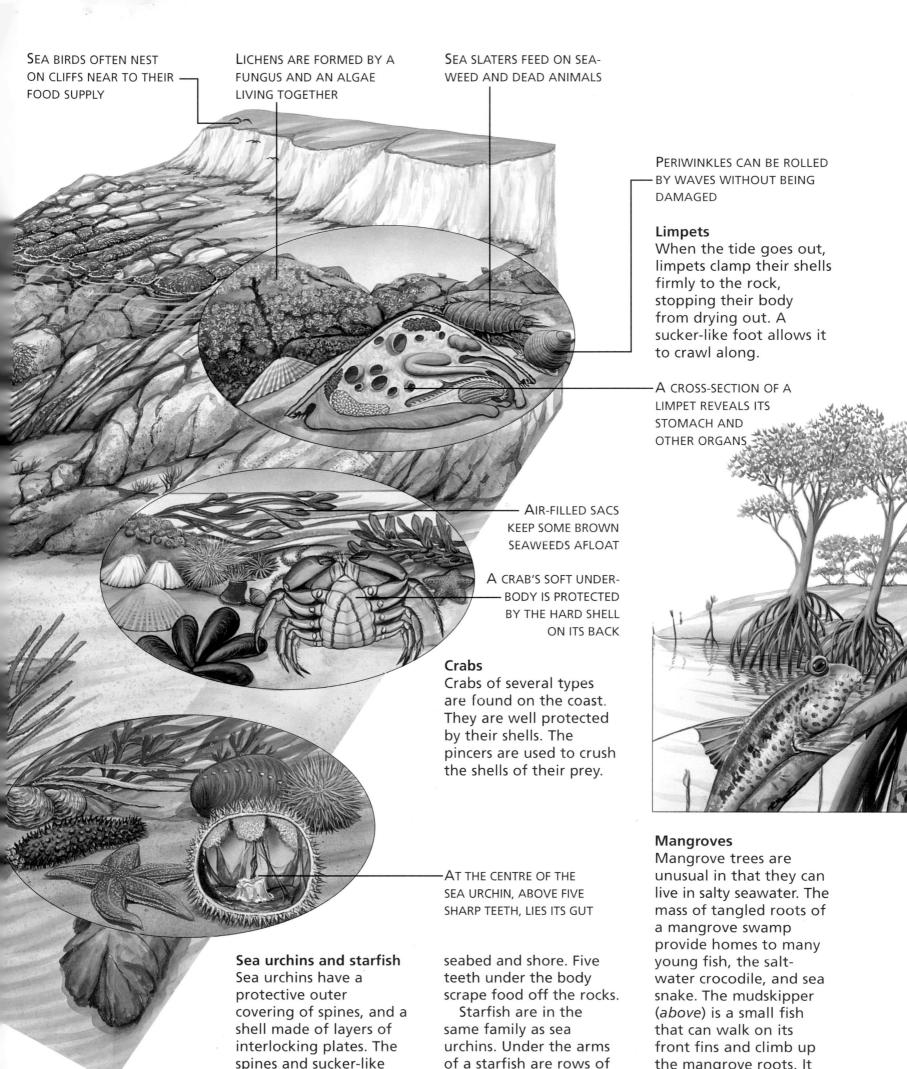

SEA BIRDS OFTEN NEST ON CLIFFS NEAR TO THEIR FOOD SUPPLY

LICHENS ARE FORMED BY A FUNGUS AND AN ALGAE LIVING TOGETHER

SEA SLATERS FEED ON SEA-WEED AND DEAD ANIMALS

PERIWINKLES CAN BE ROLLED BY WAVES WITHOUT BEING DAMAGED

Limpets
When the tide goes out, limpets clamp their shells firmly to the rock, stopping their body from drying out. A sucker-like foot allows it to crawl along.

A CROSS-SECTION OF A LIMPET REVEALS ITS STOMACH AND OTHER ORGANS

AIR-FILLED SACS KEEP SOME BROWN SEAWEEDS AFLOAT

A CRAB'S SOFT UNDER-BODY IS PROTECTED BY THE HARD SHELL ON ITS BACK

Crabs
Crabs of several types are found on the coast. They are well protected by their shells. The pincers are used to crush the shells of their prey.

AT THE CENTRE OF THE SEA URCHIN, ABOVE FIVE SHARP TEETH, LIES ITS GUT

Sea urchins and starfish
Sea urchins have a protective outer covering of spines, and a shell made of layers of interlocking plates. The spines and sucker-like feet allow urchins to move around on the seabed and shore. Five teeth under the body scrape food off the rocks.

Starfish are in the same family as sea urchins. Under the arms of a starfish are rows of tube-like feet, used for moving and feeding.

Mangroves
Mangrove trees are unusual in that they can live in salty seawater. The mass of tangled roots of a mangrove swamp provide homes to many young fish, the salt-water crocodile, and sea snake. The mudskipper (*above*) is a small fish that can walk on its front fins and climb up the mangrove roots. It feeds on small animals in the mud at low tide.

Seabirds

SEABIRDS LIVE in all of the world's oceans, from the freezing waters of the Antarctic to the warmth of tropical lagoons. Some, such as the albatross and storm petrel, spend most of their lives at sea, returning to the land only once a year to breed and moult (shed old feathers).

Seabirds eat fish, squid, or plankton and they may travel thousands of kilometres to find them. To stay warm in cold seawater most birds have a lot of fat under their skin, and they have feathers which are oiled to keep them waterproof. An exception to this is the cormorant, which has to rest out of the water with its wings outstretched to dry in the sun.

While seabirds have few natural enemies, many are killed accidentally by humans – by becoming tangled in fishing nets, or by pollution.

The brown pelican
Brown pelicans live in coastal areas of the USA. They have a large baggy pouch on the underside of their beak with which they catch lots of small fish.

The pelican flies about looking for fish which are swimming near the water surface. When a shoal of fish is spotted, the bird dives gracefully into the water, taking the fish by surprise. The pelican swims around, scooping the fish into its pouch, then returns to the surface to swallow them.

THE BROWN PELICAN FLIES SEVERAL METRES ABOVE THE SURFACE LOOKING FOR FISH

AS IT SPOTS A GROUP OF FISH CLOSE TO THE SURFACE, IT DIVES INTO THE SEA, FOLDING AWAY ITS WINGS

THE STORM PETREL HOVERS JUST ABOVE THE SURFACE

ONCE IN THE WATER THE PELICAN SCOOPS UP AS MANY FISH AS POSSIBLE

THE AUK USES ITS STUMPY WINGS TO FLY UNDERWATER

FISH SLIDE HEAD FIRST DOWN THE PELICAN'S GULLET

THE FISH THEN TRAVEL ON TOWARDS THE STOMACH

Feeding

There are many ways to catch seafood. Skimmers fly low over the surface at night using the tip of their beak to scoop up small fish and shrimps.

The storm petrel hovers over the sea surface, picking up individual fish. The auk, from the family that includes the puffin, guillemot, and razorbill, dives under the sea to chase fish using its powerful, stumpy wings and webbed feet. The albatross glides effortlessly, landing occasionally to catch fish or squid from the surface.

ALBATROSSES CATCH FISH WHILE FLOATING ON THE SURFACE

THE BLUE-FOOTED BOOBY HAS A SHALLOW DIVING ANGLE

SKIMMERS FLY FROM DUSK TO DAWN, SCOOPING UP FOOD FROM THE SURFACE

THE CORMORANT HAS A STEEP, STREAMLINED DIVE AND USES ITS FEET TO PUSH IT THROUGH THE WATER

PENGUINS CATCH FISH AND SQUID BY SWIMMING QUICKLY UNDERWATER

FISH, SQUID, AND PLANKTON ARE FOOD FOR SEABIRDS

Puffin nest
Puffins live in noisy groups on isolated islands away from land predators like rats and foxes. They nest inside tunnels, amongst rocks, or in abandoned rabbit burrows. Puffins can dig their own burrows, using their sharp claws and feet.

Kittiwake nest
Kittiwakes attach their cup-shaped nests into narrow cliff-side ledges using droppings as a kind of glue.

Guillemot nest
Guillemots nest on rock ledges, with a sheer drop to the sea below. They lay pointed eggs which are less likely to fall off if they are accidentally knocked.

Coral Reefs

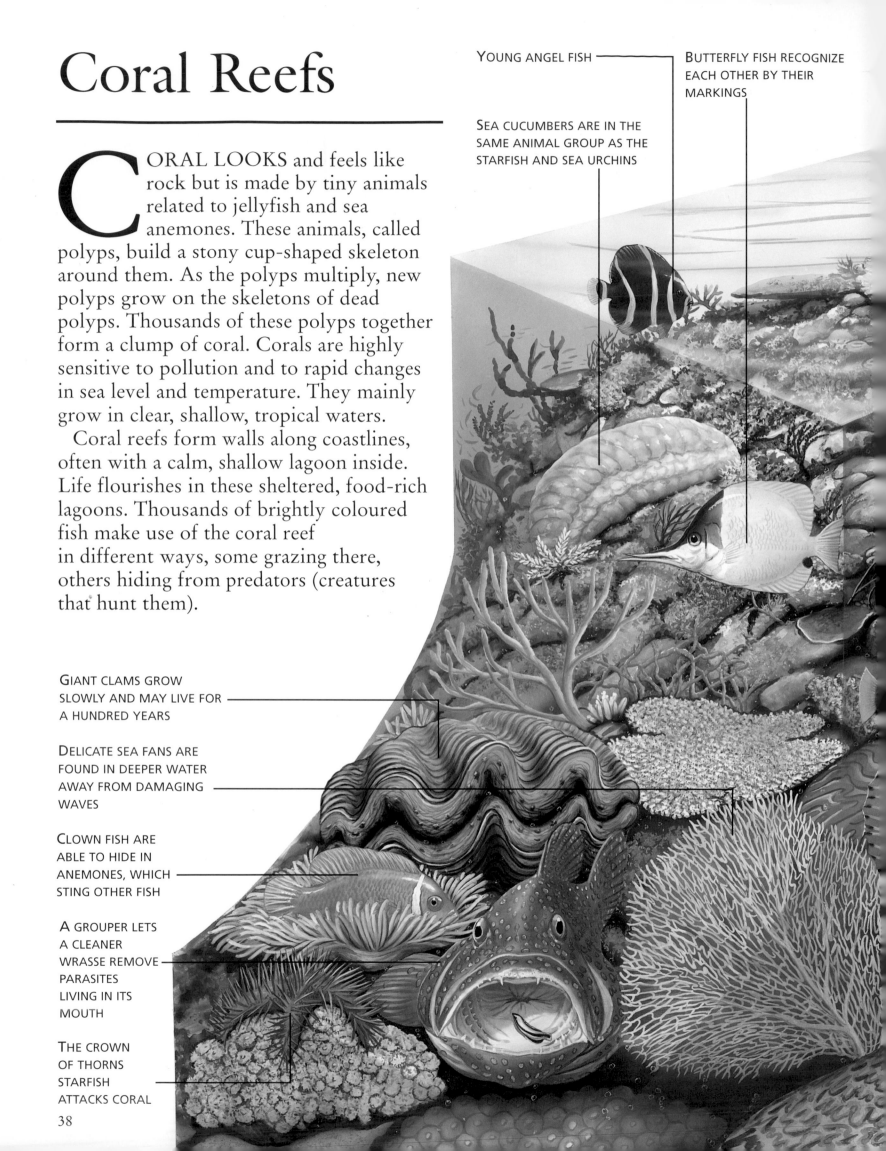

CORAL LOOKS and feels like rock but is made by tiny animals related to jellyfish and sea anemones. These animals, called polyps, build a stony cup-shaped skeleton around them. As the polyps multiply, new polyps grow on the skeletons of dead polyps. Thousands of these polyps together form a clump of coral. Corals are highly sensitive to pollution and to rapid changes in sea level and temperature. They mainly grow in clear, shallow, tropical waters.

Coral reefs form walls along coastlines, often with a calm, shallow lagoon inside. Life flourishes in these sheltered, food-rich lagoons. Thousands of brightly coloured fish make use of the coral reef in different ways, some grazing there, others hiding from predators (creatures that hunt them).

YOUNG ANGEL FISH

BUTTERFLY FISH RECOGNIZE EACH OTHER BY THEIR MARKINGS

SEA CUCUMBERS ARE IN THE SAME ANIMAL GROUP AS THE STARFISH AND SEA URCHINS

GIANT CLAMS GROW SLOWLY AND MAY LIVE FOR A HUNDRED YEARS

DELICATE SEA FANS ARE FOUND IN DEEPER WATER AWAY FROM DAMAGING WAVES

CLOWN FISH ARE ABLE TO HIDE IN ANEMONES, WHICH STING OTHER FISH

A GROUPER LETS A CLEANER WRASSE REMOVE PARASITES LIVING IN ITS MOUTH

THE CROWN OF THORNS STARFISH ATTACKS CORAL

MORE KINDS OF FISH CAN BE SEEN ON A REEF THAN IN ANY OTHER HABITAT IN THE SEA

THE POLYP'S MOUTH

A STONY BASE ANCHORS THE POLYP

PLATE-LIKE CORALS CAN SURVIVE IN THE MORE TURBULENT SURFACE WATERS

TROPICAL SLUGS EXIST IN A VARIETY OF BRIGHT COLOURS

STAGHORN CORALS USED TO BE TAKEN AND SOLD, BUT ARE NOW PROTECTED BY THE LAWS OF SOME COUNTRIES

ANGEL FISH CHANGE PATTERN AS THEY GROW INTO ADULTS – THIS IS AN ADULT ANGEL FISH

ALTHOUGH BEAUTIFUL, THE REEF CAN BE A DANGEROUS PLACE FOR HUMANS – MANY OF THE ANIMALS HAVE PAINFUL SPINES AND STRONG STINGS

THE LION FISH HAS POISONOUS SPINES PROTECTING ITS BACK

BRAIN CORALS GROW SLOWLY AND HAVE ANNUAL GROWTH RINGS LIKE A TREE

Coral polyp

The polyp is supported in a stone-like cup. It makes the cup from substances dissolved in seawater. The cup, called a theca, anchors the polyp to the older layers below and to the polyps around it.

The tentacles catch food, although the coral gets most of its food from tiny single-celled plants that live inside the coral's tissues.

How coral atolls form

A coral reef starts to grow around a volcanic island (1). The volcano becomes inactive and erodes away or sinks while the reef keeps growing (2). When the island has sunk completely, the reef appears ring- or horseshoe-shaped from above. It has a shallow lagoon in the middle (3).

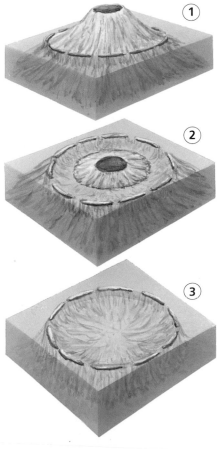

① ② ③

Ocean Pollution

ALMOST ALL rivers and drainage systems eventually flow into the ocean, carrying waste products from human activities out to sea. The ocean has become an enormous sink for chemicals, sewage, and rubbish as a result of wars, accidents, and deliberate dumping. Of course the ocean is very large, and not all pollutants (polluting substances) cause major problems. Bacteria exist which will eat up oil spills, or even digest steel, and over many years the ocean can clean itself very well. But where pollutants are concentrated, a great deal of damage can be done. Coastal waters beside large cities, intensively farmed land, or heavy industries can become so polluted that natural systems cannot cope. The result can be death for marine life, ugly pollution along coastlines, and damage to the health of the human population.

Today, research is being done to find out how much waste can be safely allowed into the oceans. Many countries are trying to control pollution.

Poisonous waters

There are so many sources of pollution that it is difficult to know exactly what is being poured into the sea. Chemicals that are harmless on their own get mixed with others and produce dangerous mixtures that can have unexpected effects, such as turning male fish into females. Nutrients (food) in sewage and fertilizers (crop sprays) can make poisonous plankton grow at an alarming rate, causing plankton blooms, or red tides.

SOME OF THE CHEMICALS SPRAYED ON CROPS END UP IN RIVERS AND OCEANS

HOUSING DEVELOPMENTS NEAR THE COAST INCREASE LOCAL POLLUTION LEVELS

SEWERS CAN LEAK INTO GROUNDWATER AND SPOIL WATER SUPPLIES

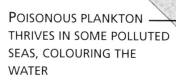

POISONOUS PLANKTON THRIVES IN SOME POLLUTED SEAS, COLOURING THE WATER

SEWAGE SLUDGE DUMPED FROM A SHIP IS POISONOUS TO MARINE LIFE

DUMPED MINING WASTE CAN POISON THE WATER, SMOTHER THE SEA FLOOR, AND KILL MARINE LIFE

Fertilizer damage

Farmers use large quantities of artificial fertilizer so that they can grow as many crops as possible. Some of the fertilizer gets washed into rivers by rainfall, and carried into coastal waters where the local marine plants start growing at a greater rate. The fast-growing plants can choke the spaces where other animals and plants would normally live, and when the plants start to rot they begin to smell and attract many insects.

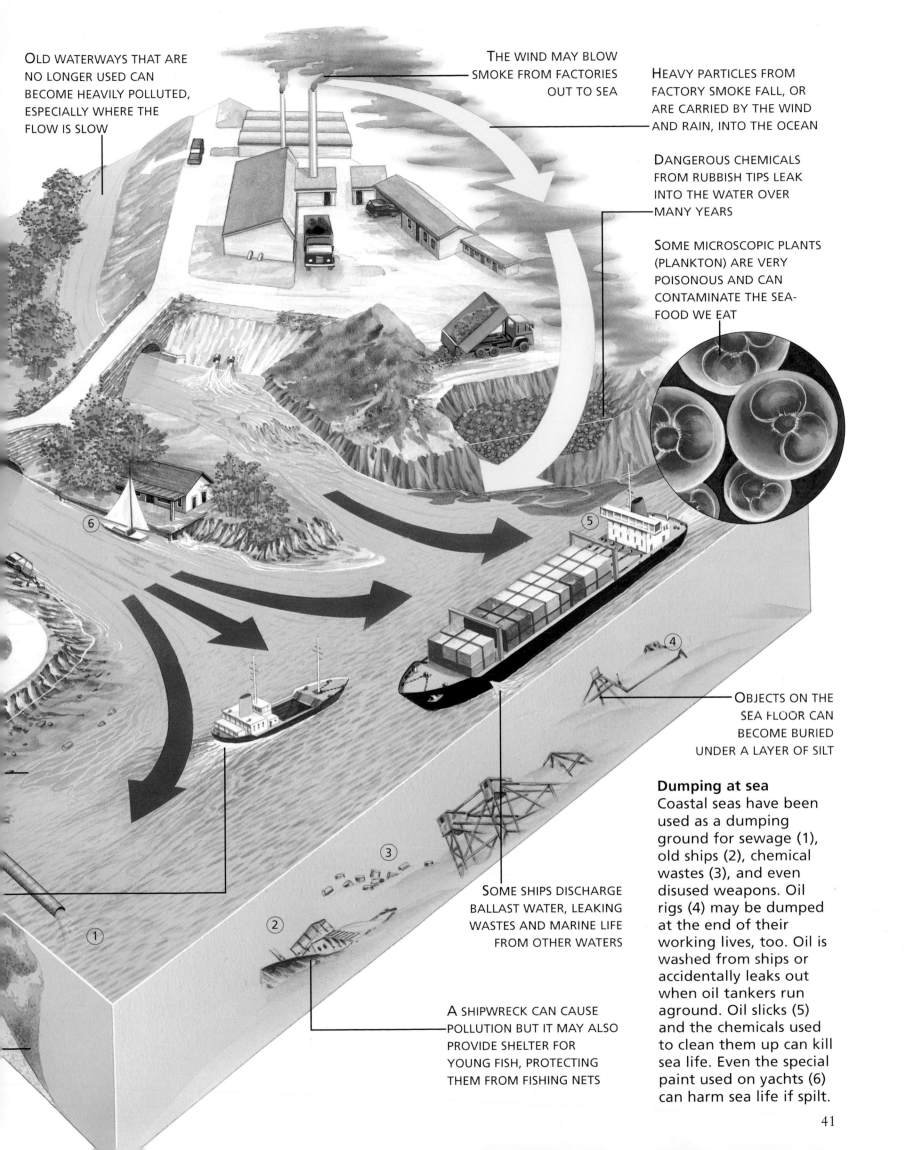

OLD WATERWAYS THAT ARE NO LONGER USED CAN BECOME HEAVILY POLLUTED, ESPECIALLY WHERE THE FLOW IS SLOW

THE WIND MAY BLOW SMOKE FROM FACTORIES OUT TO SEA

HEAVY PARTICLES FROM FACTORY SMOKE FALL, OR ARE CARRIED BY THE WIND AND RAIN, INTO THE OCEAN

DANGEROUS CHEMICALS FROM RUBBISH TIPS LEAK INTO THE WATER OVER MANY YEARS

SOME MICROSCOPIC PLANTS (PLANKTON) ARE VERY POISONOUS AND CAN CONTAMINATE THE SEA-FOOD WE EAT

OBJECTS ON THE SEA FLOOR CAN BECOME BURIED UNDER A LAYER OF SILT

SOME SHIPS DISCHARGE BALLAST WATER, LEAKING WASTES AND MARINE LIFE FROM OTHER WATERS

A SHIPWRECK CAN CAUSE POLLUTION BUT IT MAY ALSO PROVIDE SHELTER FOR YOUNG FISH, PROTECTING THEM FROM FISHING NETS

Dumping at sea
Coastal seas have been used as a dumping ground for sewage (1), old ships (2), chemical wastes (3), and even disused weapons. Oil rigs (4) may be dumped at the end of their working lives, too. Oil is washed from ships or accidentally leaks out when oil tankers run aground. Oil slicks (5) and the chemicals used to clean them up can kill sea life. Even the special paint used on yachts (6) can harm sea life if spilt.

Mining the Sea

BENEATH THE ocean floor there are vast reserves of oil, gas, and coal, as well as other minerals and metals that are of value to humans. The ocean floor has valuable reserves of sand and gravel which can be used in road building and construction. Occasionally the sand and gravel contains diamonds or other precious substances.

Where a resource is in plentiful supply on land, like coal for example, there is not much point in mining it from beneath the sea. However, oil and gas are so valuable that the difficulty and cost of drilling exploration wells, building offshore platforms, and sending reserves to the shore are thought to be worth while.

In the future, as reserves of raw materials run out on the land, other products will be mined from the sea.

FLARE STACK BURNS OFF EXCESS GAS

Oil platform
The superstructure is built of several modules, which are lifted onto the jacket by cranes. There are modules for power, engineering, pump rooms, accommodation, catering, medical services, and entertainment.

A PIPE FROM THIS DERRICK CARRIES OIL AND GAS TO THE SURFACE

GAS TURBINE EXHAUSTS

THE STEEL JACKET (FRAMEWORK) IS REGULARLY MAINTAINED BY DIVERS AND UNDERWATER ROBOTS

CONSTANT RAIN OF ORGANIC MATERIAL ONTO SEABED

INCREASING PRESSURE AND TEMPERATURE GRADUALLY CAUSE HYDROCARBONS TO FORM

Formation of oil and gas
Organic matter such as plankton drifts to the seabed and gets buried (*top right*). Over time the layers of decomposing matter deepen, and their temperature and pressure increase. Chemical reactions and bacteria slowly change the organic matter into hydrocarbons such as oil and gas (*middle*). Along geological faults the oil and gas may get trapped behind layers of rock (*bottom*).

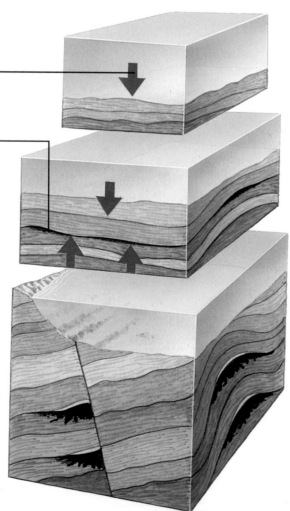

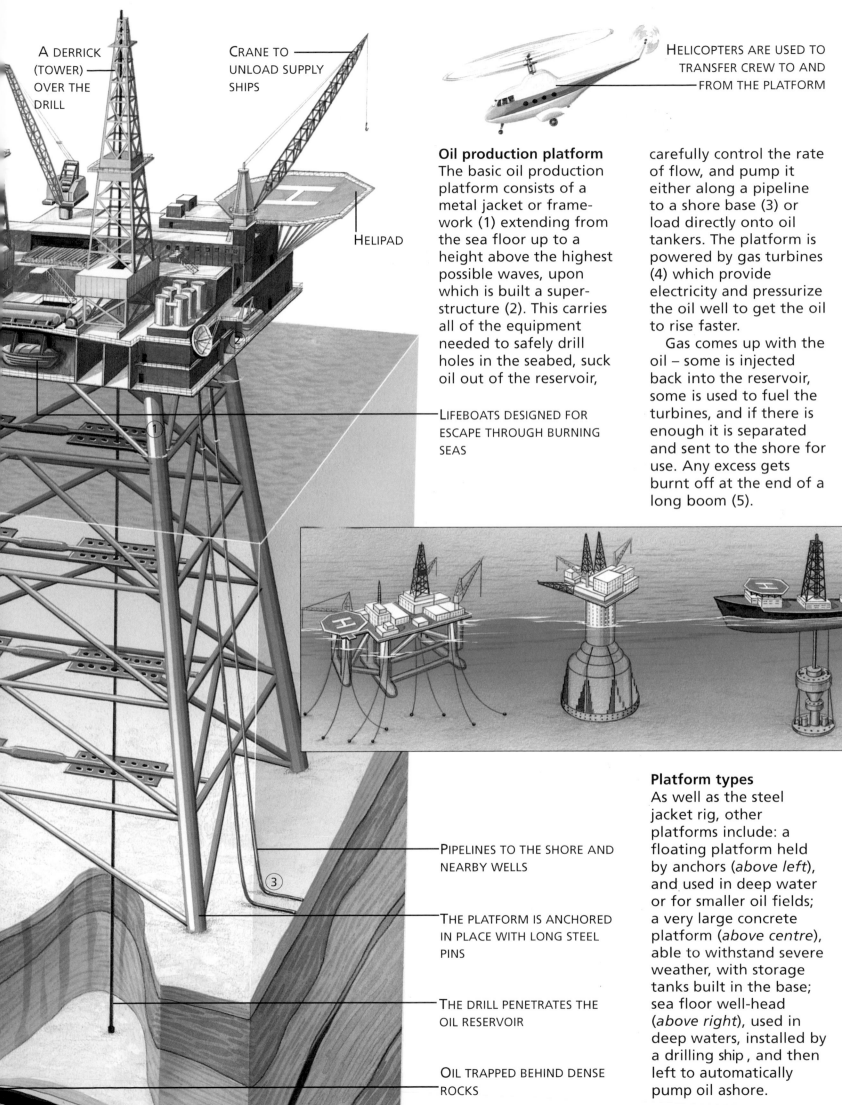

A DERRICK (TOWER) OVER THE DRILL

CRANE TO UNLOAD SUPPLY SHIPS

HELICOPTERS ARE USED TO TRANSFER CREW TO AND FROM THE PLATFORM

HELIPAD

Oil production platform

The basic oil production platform consists of a metal jacket or frame-work (1) extending from the sea floor up to a height above the highest possible waves, upon which is built a super-structure (2). This carries all of the equipment needed to safely drill holes in the seabed, suck oil out of the reservoir, carefully control the rate of flow, and pump it either along a pipeline to a shore base (3) or load directly onto oil tankers. The platform is powered by gas turbines (4) which provide electricity and pressurize the oil well to get the oil to rise faster.

Gas comes up with the oil – some is injected back into the reservoir, some is used to fuel the turbines, and if there is enough it is separated and sent to the shore for use. Any excess gets burnt off at the end of a long boom (5).

LIFEBOATS DESIGNED FOR ESCAPE THROUGH BURNING SEAS

PIPELINES TO THE SHORE AND NEARBY WELLS

THE PLATFORM IS ANCHORED IN PLACE WITH LONG STEEL PINS

THE DRILL PENETRATES THE OIL RESERVOIR

OIL TRAPPED BEHIND DENSE ROCKS

Platform types

As well as the steel jacket rig, other platforms include: a floating platform held by anchors (*above left*), and used in deep water or for smaller oil fields; a very large concrete platform (*above centre*), able to withstand severe weather, with storage tanks built in the base; sea floor well-head (*above right*), used in deep waters, installed by a drilling ship , and then left to automatically pump oil ashore.

Ocean Power

THE SEA provides huge amounts of energy which can be used to generate electricity in ways that do not cause pollution or release any gases which can change the climate. And power from the sea will never run out. So why has it taken so long to develop this power? The answer is that people have thought that the cost of setting up the machinery is too high. Large, complex machines need to be built, then towed out to rough waters and moored in position. It would be many years before the sale of power would cover the cost of building and installing the machines, and even longer before any profit was made. But now the threat of pollution is being taken much more seriously and alternative forms of energy, such as sea power, are being used.

Thermal power

Ocean Thermal Energy Conversion (OTEC) uses the difference in temperature between warm surface water and deep cold water to evaporate liquid ammonia and spin a turbine electrical generator. It works best in the tropics where the cold water can be piped to nearby islands after use.

The picture (*right*) and diagram (*below, right*) show how the system works. Warm surface water boils liquid ammonia to make it into a vapour (1). The ammonia vapour spins a turbine to make electricity (2). Very cold water is drawn up from deep in the ocean (3), and condenses the ammonia back into liquid (4). The liquid travels back to the tank (5) to be used over and over again.

CROSS-SECTION OF A THERMAL POWER PLANT

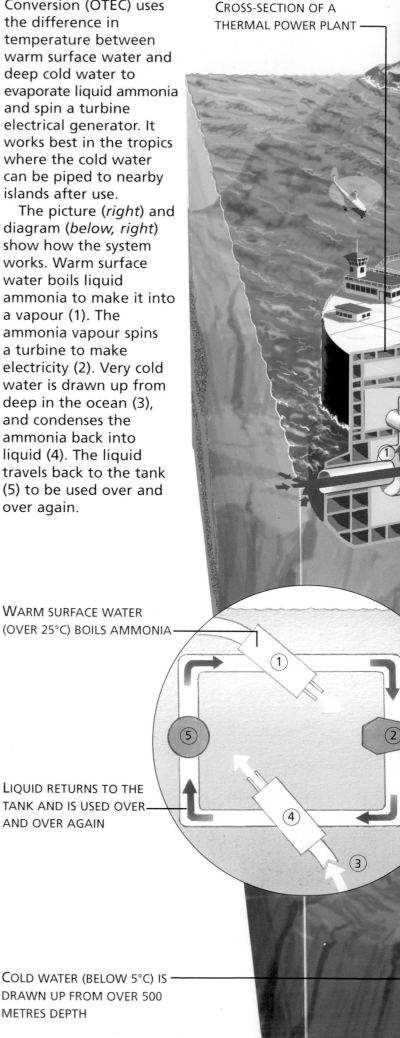

WARM SURFACE WATER (OVER 25°C) BOILS AMMONIA

LIQUID RETURNS TO THE TANK AND IS USED OVER AND OVER AGAIN

COLD WATER (BELOW 5°C) IS DRAWN UP FROM OVER 500 METRES DEPTH

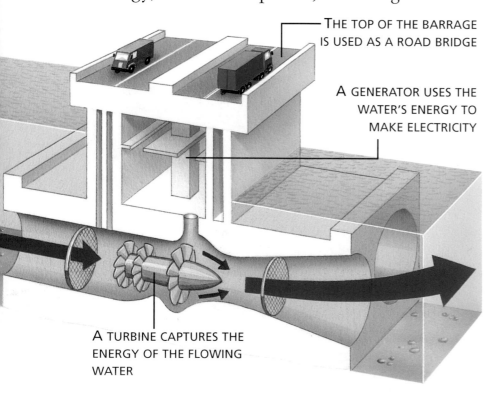

THE TOP OF THE BARRAGE IS USED AS A ROAD BRIDGE

A GENERATOR USES THE WATER'S ENERGY TO MAKE ELECTRICITY

A TURBINE CAPTURES THE ENERGY OF THE FLOWING WATER

Tidal power barrage

People first used sea power by building dams across estuaries. At high tide the estuary would fill up. At low tide the water was released, passing across a water wheel geared to a mill for grinding grain. In today's version, called a tidal power barrage, the water spins a turbine to make electricity.

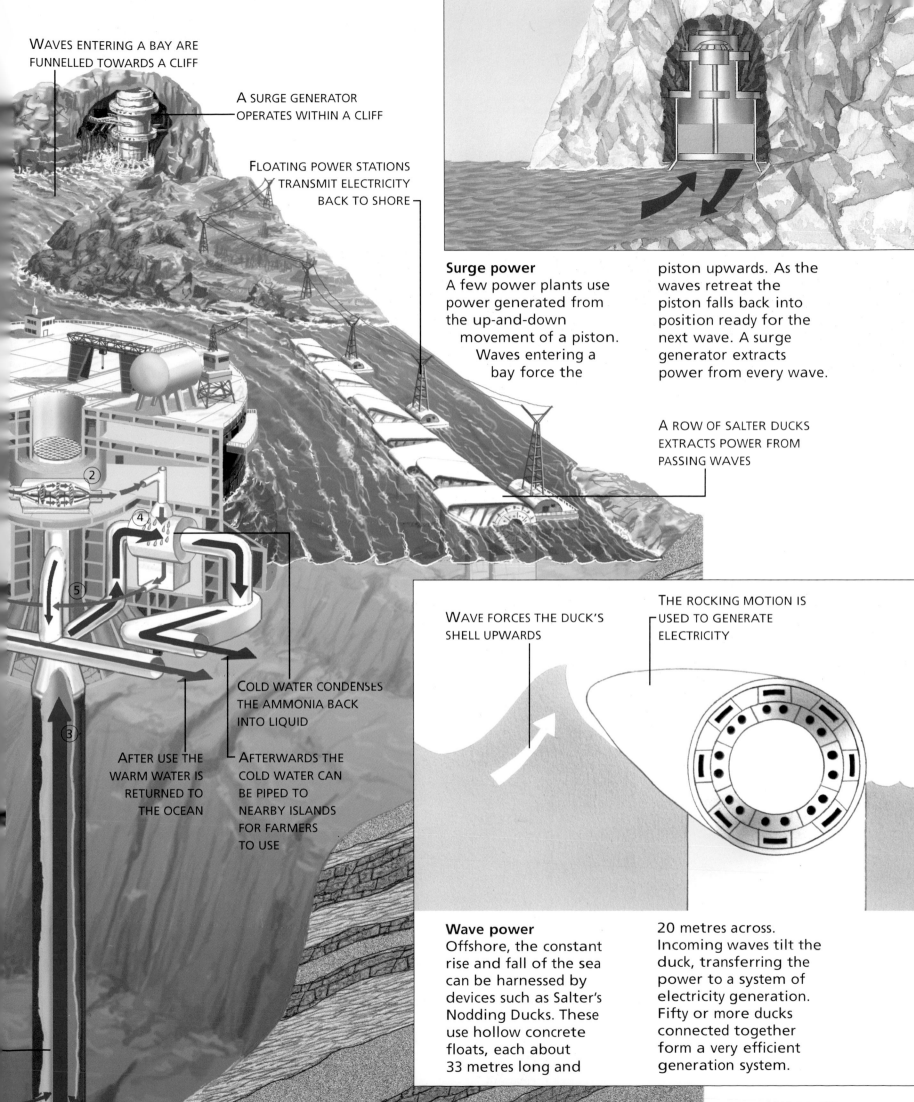

WAVES ENTERING A BAY ARE
FUNNELLED TOWARDS A CLIFF

A SURGE GENERATOR
OPERATES WITHIN A CLIFF

FLOATING POWER STATIONS
TRANSMIT ELECTRICITY
BACK TO SHORE

Surge power
A few power plants use power generated from the up-and-down movement of a piston. Waves entering a bay force the piston upwards. As the waves retreat the piston falls back into position ready for the next wave. A surge generator extracts power from every wave.

A ROW OF SALTER DUCKS
EXTRACTS POWER FROM
PASSING WAVES

COLD WATER CONDENSES
THE AMMONIA BACK
INTO LIQUID

AFTER USE THE
WARM WATER IS
RETURNED TO
THE OCEAN

AFTERWARDS THE
COLD WATER CAN
BE PIPED TO
NEARBY ISLANDS
FOR FARMERS
TO USE

WAVE FORCES THE DUCK'S
SHELL UPWARDS

THE ROCKING MOTION IS
USED TO GENERATE
ELECTRICITY

Wave power
Offshore, the constant rise and fall of the sea can be harnessed by devices such as Salter's Nodding Ducks. These use hollow concrete floats, each about 33 metres long and 20 metres across. Incoming waves tilt the duck, transferring the power to a system of electricity generation. Fifty or more ducks connected together form a very efficient generation system.

Index